Marco Improta
Italian Government Instability

De Gruyter
Disruptions

Volume 5

Marco Improta

Italian Government Instability

Roots, Drivers, and Remedies

DE GRUYTER

ISBN 978-3-11-132966-6
e-ISBN (PDF) 978-3-11-132972-7
e-ISBN (EPUB) 978-3-11-132978-9
ISSN 2748-9086

Library of Congress Control Number: 2025934890

Bibliographic information published by the Deutsche Nationalbibliothek
The Deutsche Nationalbibliothek lists this publication in the Deutsche Nationalbibliografie;
detailed bibliographic data are available on the internet at http://dnb.dnb.de.

www.degruyter.com
Questions about General Product Safety Regulation:
productsafety@degruyterbrill.com

To my family

Contents

Introduction —— 1

Chapter 1
Rationale, objectives, and strategies —— 5

Chapter 2
A past still present: At the roots of government instability —— 15

Chapter 3
Italy in a longitudinal and comparative perspective —— 27

Chapter 4
Who did what? Government instability and policymaking
accountability —— 47

Chapter 5
Explanatory drivers: Between party conflicts and general
vulnerability —— 63

Chapter 6
How to solve instability? Institutional remedies and policy
recommendations —— 69

Conclusion —— 81

References —— 87

Appendix: Data codebook —— 93

Index —— 103

Introduction

Government instability is a defining feature of Italian politics, which has had far-reaching implications for the country's democratic quality as well as policymaking effectiveness. Since the establishment of the Italian Republic in 1946, the political system has been marked by frequent cabinet turnovers, fragile coalition governments, and party system fragmentation. These features have often been seen as critical barriers to effective governance, and although several other countries have experienced the same phenomena, Italy has had some of the shortest-lived governments in Europe (e.g., King et al., 1990).

This book aims to explore the roots of government instability, the factors that contribute to it, and potential remedies to address the issues. I employ a three-step analysis. First, I trace the historical origins of government instability in Italy, as understanding the trajectories of this phenomenon provides valuable insights. Second, I empirically assess the impact of key factors in explaining both short and long government durations. Third, I adopt an approach that can be described as "applied political science," as I aim to be constructive by proposing potential solutions to government instability.

Considering the historical roots of instability, the issue can be traced back to the immediate post-war period, when the newly formed Republic sought to establish a democratic system after decades of fascist rule under Benito Mussolini. The constitution of 1948, which laid the foundation for Italy's democratic institutions, was designed to prevent the rise of authoritarianism by dispersing power among several political actors (and also other institutional ones). This, however, came at the cost of stability, as the proportional representation (PR) electoral system encouraged the proliferation of small parties equipped with fundamental veto powers (Tsebelis, 1995), making it difficult for single parties to gain a majority. During the First Republic (1948–1992), Italian governments were indeed characterized by short durations and frequent changes in the driving seat of Palazzo Chigi, primarily due to the highly fragmented nature of the party system. The predominance of Christian Democracy (DC), which held power for much of this period, was counterbalanced by the necessity of forming broad coalitions with smaller parties (for instance, liberals and socialists). As a result, Italian governments struggled to maintain satisfactory policy continuity and coherence, frequently collapsing due to internal conflicts. The transition (for some authors still incomplete, see Pasquino, 2023) to the Second Republic in the early 1990s, precipitated by a series of corruption scandals known as *Tangentopoli*, brought about significant reforms aimed at reducing fragmentation and enhancing government stability. These re-

https://doi.org/10.1515/9783111329727-001

forms included changes to the electoral system, which introduced a mixed-member PR model, and efforts to curb political corruption. However, despite these reforms, government instability persisted, albeit in a slightly less severe form (as we will observe in more detail in this book). The emergence of new political actors started to become evident, such as Silvio Berlusconi's Forza Italia and later the Five Star Movement (M5S). Such parties introduced new incentives but also new challenges to coalition-building and cabinet governance. Finally, the Third Republic (beginning in the 2010s) has been similarly affected by high levels of fragmentation, as the rise of new political movements and the continued weakening of mainstream parties have exacerbated the difficulties of forming predictable patterns of party interaction in the governmental arena. The repeated collapse of coalition governments, such as those led by Matteo Renzi and Giuseppe Conte, underscores the enduring nature of Italian government instability – a problem that has accompanied all eras of Italian republican history.

While Italy's experience with government instability is often considered peculiar, it is not entirely unique. Other democracies, particularly those with PR electoral systems, have also faced challenges related to stability in office. Countries like Israel, Belgium, France (Fourth Republic), and the Netherlands have experienced similar difficulties in forming stable governments due to the need to accommodate multiple parties with often divergent interests and political goals. In Israel, for example, government instability has been a recurring issue since the establishment of the state in 1948. Like Italy's, the Israeli political system is characterized by a high degree of fragmentation, with many small parties vying for influence in coalition governments. This has led to frequent elections (eliciting voter fatigue issues – see Garmann, 2017) and the premature ends of governments. Belgium, another fragmented democratic model, has also witnessed problems of instability in government, particularly due to its complex federal structure and linguistic divisions. The need to balance the interests of the Flemish and Walloon communities has made coalition-building and bargaining a protracted and often contentious process. Thus, if we adopt a comparative perspective, Italy should not be regarded as a peculiar case. By comparing Italy's conditions with that of other democracies, this book draws lessons from cases of success and failure, which helps advance some potential remedies for the issues.

Along these lines, a key focus of this book is the role that institutional design plays in shaping government stability. The design of Italy's electoral and political institutions has been central to the country's recurring issues with government instability. Therefore, in this book I stress the critical role of proportional representation, fragmentation, lack of party discipline, and the absence of effective mechanisms for managing coalition conflicts. All these factors have aggravated government instability in the country. For example, the inability to impose binding coalition agreements has allowed parties to defect from coalitions or pursue policies that are at odds with their partners (see, for instance, the case of the first Conte government over economic and labor reform), leading to frequent government crises (Capati et al., 2023). Moreover, the lack of a constructive vote of no confidence, which requires that a new government be formed before an existing one can be dissolved, has made it easier for opposition parties to bring down governments without offering a viable alternative.

To examine government instability in Italy, this book employs a range of quantitative and qualitative methods. The survival analysis used in this book is based on an original dataset covering Italian governments from 1948. I use Cox proportional hazards models to investigate the risks associated with government survival, aligning with standard methodologies (King et al., 1990). In addition to survival analysis, the book draws on document analysis, to trace how institutional mechanisms have contributed to increasing instability in the country.

The book scrutinizes the roots of government instability in Italy. The historical roots of the instability issue start from the poor cohesiveness identifiable in the nation-building process of the country. I also examine the features which accompanied the installation of the Italian Republic in 1948. I outline how the proportional representation electoral system and the fear of excessive governmental power contributed to creating short-lived cabinets, especially during the First Republic. Specifically, the constitutional framers, seeking to prevent the reemergence of authoritarian experiences in government, designed a political system that diffuses power across multiple actors, inadvertently laying the groundwork for fragmentation. In this book, I put Italy in comparative perspective by comparing the Italian experience with other post-war democracies, particularly those that also adopted proportional representation and power-sharing provisions.

Moreover, I examine the diffusion and attribution of responsibility among governing parties regarding specific policies, distinguishing between policy initiators and political actors involved in the implementation phases of the same policy. This analysis is useful for understanding whether and how government instability in Italy may explain the poor performance in producing effective public policies. My assumption is that if a given policy is designed and envisioned by a political actor with preference X, the policy risks being carried out suboptimally in the subsequent stages if the political actor changes and brings in preference Y.

Having explored the issues presented, Chapter 5 is dedicated to a survival analysis where I investigate the impact of party conflicts and general vulnerability on the risk associated with governments facing premature termination. In light of the results obtained in Chapter 5, the following chapter suggests some remedies to address the issue of instability. Clearly, the most effective remedy for government instability in any political system is the development of a robust political culture of cooperation, which can shield the system from threats posed by fragmentation and institutions that are not designed to foster the emergence of stable governing coalitions.

Finally, the book concludes with a section where the key findings from this research are discussed, expressing hope for a future marked by greater stability in Italian governments.

Chapter 1
Rationale, objectives, and strategies

This chapter explains the rationale behind the investigation of government instability in Italy and abroad, why we should care about this topic, and the scientific debate around this issue. The chapter continues by explaining the objectives of the book and the strategies envisaged to properly examine government instability.

1 Government instability as a democratic problem

Modern democracies are getting harder and harder to govern. In many countries, the proportion of administrations that fall short of their constitutionally mandated term limits is rising (Improta, 2023). Regardless of the type of government or democratic model (Lijphart, 1999), this phenomenon has impacted many national settings. For instance, in Israel's recent political developments – a consensus democracy – government instability has been a defining feature. This has led to a political impasse in which three government heads – Netanyahu, Bennett, and Lapid – were sworn in and served for an average of just over a year (Rahat & Hazan, 2022). In just under four years, Israeli citizens were asked to cast ballots five times (Shamir & Rahat, 2022).

Consensus democracies have not been the only ones to experience problems with government instability. In fact, the recent, frenetic turnover of governments in the United Kingdom – the quintessential majoritarian democratic model ("Westminster") – has sparked unprecedented government crises, such as those resulting from the resignation of Boris Johnson and the formation of the Truss cabinet during the interelection period. But after just 44 days in power, Truss was compelled to step down due to growing unrest in the political and financial arenas, making her the British prime minister with the shortest tenure ever. Following the termination of this administration, Rishi Sunak, another Conservative Party member, took the oath of office as prime minister (Improta & Mannoni, 2024).

Italy has historically been thought of as a country with frequent cabinet changes and high levels of political instability (Mershon, 1996; Cotta & Marangoni, 2015). The importance of the instability issue in Italy has been further reaffirmed by recent political events: three distinct cabinets (Conte I, Conte II, and Draghi) were formed within the 2018–2022 parliamentary period. Italy has had three political crises since 2019. In particular, League and Italy Alive – junior partners with important blackmail potential (Sartori, 1976) – withdrew their support from Conte I

https://doi.org/10.1515/9783111329727-002

and Conte II, respectively, leading to the termination of both Conte governments. Ultimately, the national unity government led by Mario Draghi, the former president of the European Central Bank, collapsed due to internal tensions that mostly derived from Conte's doubts about the government's military support for Ukraine to counter the 2022 Russian invasion of Ukraine.

Leaders and governments in democratic systems face a variety of difficulties in addition to "simple" lawmaking in an environment of heightened pressure and unrest from both domestic and international arenas. Prime ministers and cabinet members deal with several challenges during a democratic cabinet's life cycle, including shifts in public opinion preferences, media and opposition scrutiny of governmental performance, and external shocks and events like international and health crises and military conflicts. As Italy contributes to the European integration process as a founding member of the European Union (EU), policy and reform-making in Italy must be coordinated with European institutions under an interconnected, cooperative framework (Fabbrini & Piattoni, 2008). This task is not simple. Governments may face a "responsibility vs. responsiveness" conundrum, as Mair (2009) pointed out, which may alter the effectiveness of policymaking. This is because, on the one hand, leaders who focus on the responsive side deal with the risk of not meeting the standards of responsible governance (informally) set by globalized markets and supranational organizations like the EU. However, focusing on responsibility might increase risks regarding satisfying citizens' demands and needs.

The deeply ingrained crises that political parties in European democracies are going through are made worse by all this complexity. Political science literature, for instance, has documented the persistent decline in party membership (e.g., Van Biezen et al., 2012), the increasing distrust of political parties and other actors and institutions (e.g., Bertsou, 2019), the growing reliance on non-elected representatives in national governments (e.g., Emanuele et al., 2023), the decline in voter turnout, particularly among youth (e.g., Angelucci et al., 2024), and the unstable nature of party interactions in various contexts (e.g., Chiaramonte & Emanuele, 2022). These occurrences collectively constitute a few "red flags" signaling the poor health of modern democracies (Improta, 2022b).

Furthermore, the task of governing becomes more complex when macro- and micro-trends are combined. How can Italian governments handle all this complexity if their average duration is only one year? How can long-term planning and implementation of policies be accomplished with such a short time horizon? If the main priority of ruling parties running for reelection is short-termism, how can the needs and demands of both current and future generations be considered? Time is needed for effective governance. Governments require time to formulate effective policies and manage pressing issues. Put differently, governments require stability in their life cycle, ideally reaching the end term stipulated by the constitution.

Unstable administrations typically record subpar performance, as Huber (1998) contended. According to some scholars, unstable cabinets can jeopardize a democracy's ability to function (Warwick, 1994). Lijphart (1999) asserts that short-lived governments lead to systemic performance problems because they are unable to communicate and collaborate with the legislative branch in an efficient manner. Some other scholars, on the other hand, are less convinced about the effect of instability on democratic and governmental performance. For example, Sartori (1982) argued that the duration of government in office can only be regarded as an empirical referent as cabinets might remain in office for an extended period without enacting impactful policies and even acting irresponsibly. Sartori (1982) contended that stable governments may still face circumstances of "ruling immobility" about policymaking. However, recent research has documented that the likelihood of cabinet termination increases when political constraints limit the room for government-based policy change (Improta, 2024). In this book, I share the conclusion of D'Alimonte and Mammarella (2022) regarding the issue: stability alone does not guarantee effective governance, but it is a prerequisite for creating the conditions for it.

Several examples of the detrimental effects of unstable governments may be seen in the recent political developments in Italy – a country that is a prime example in this respect. As previously said, a peculiarity of the Italian political system is its tendency towards government instability. The effectiveness and reliability of the Italian government have suffered many consequences because of this "pathology." What Romano Prodi – former Italian prime minister – recalled a few years ago[1] serves as a telling illustration. Specifically, Prodi related a story about his first encounter as the leader of Italy's government with German chancellor Helmut Kohl. After the conclusion of their meeting, Kohl asked Prodi, "who is coming next time?" In this light, government reliability in international affairs is impacted by the short endurance of Italian governments, undermining the country's effectiveness in defending its interests and positions in the global scenario. Additionally, leaders in a supranational and globalized environment need to cooperatively imagine future goals, but Italian leaders must seek to impose themselves

---

1 The full video can be accessed via this link: https://video.repubblica.it/mondo/morto-kohl-prodi-al-primo-incontro-mi-chiese-la-prossima-volta-chi-viene/278777/279380.

internationally considering their potentially limited time horizon in office. Therefore, there is little doubt that instability has an impact on global cooperation and
ties. After Prodi and Kohl's meeting, some time has passed. Nonetheless, it is still
clear how unstable Italian governments are.

More generally, political scientists throughout the world have been focused on issues regarding the reasons behind the varying durations that democratic governments record (e.g., King et al., 1990). As a result, political instability quickly rose
to the top of the comparative politics agenda. The first contributions on this matter date back to Lowell (1896). Though Italy has some of the lowest levels of government duration, there are still few systematic studies that are solely focused on
examining government instability in this country (a notable exception, albeit not
focusing on stability alone, is Curini & Pinto, 2017). Scholars usually focus on the
early phases of the democratic life cycle, such as government formation. Despite
a sizable amount of literature, current research on the topic has several drawbacks. Most importantly, researchers are still reflecting on which variables primarily account for explaining longer or shorter survival in office. This complexity
stems from problems with various conceptualization, operationalization, mea-
surement, and methodological approaches (Saalfeld, 2008).

As shown in recent advances in the area, it is relevant to continue researching
the matter through the lens of the coalition life cycle (Strøm et al., 2008; Bergman
et al., 2021). Government termination is specifically interpreted by life cycle theorists as an essential step in the process that includes election, government formation, and governance. Since these stages are closely related, integrated methods
and perspectives should be used to study them. As previously indicated, signs of
future government instability may be seen from the very beginning of a government's existence and are generally viewed as essential preconditions for effective
governance. Several comparative investigations have examined this issue by including numerous examples in an all-encompassing longitudinal framework.
Quantitative statistical approaches have been the preferred instruments to analyze government instability and provide findings that could be applied broadly
when using this kind of empirical strategy. Thus, the lack of in-depth analyses
and case studies that would bolster the issue's rigorous examination and the reliability of the current findings reported in the literature is a weakness of this established research agenda. This book aims to fill this gap.

Is government instability a problem for democracy? Not every country faces this
issue, but we can confidently state that it is a major problem for Italy. Since the
country's democratic installation, government instability has arguably been a
well-known aspect of the Italian political system. Nonetheless, the issue has been

addressed in only a few research articles (Allum, 1974; Cioffi-Revilla, 1984; Mershon, 1996), which are now outdated and, as in the case of Allum (1974) and Mershon (1996), investigated the issue only tangentially. In scientific articles and books dealing with the Italian government, government instability is often depicted as a critical problem for the country, undermining its domestic (i.e., vis-à-vis the citizenry) and international reliability. The instability issue remains in the background and is interpreted as an inexorable fate. Therefore, the extant literature simply refers to government instability as a peculiarity of the Italian case without digging deeper into the factors underpinning it.

Why is government instability a democratic problem? In this book, I argue that for democracies to work well, the public needs to record high levels of trust, satisfaction, and efficacy to make political institutions and processes work (see also Dassonneville & McAllister, 2020). According to Angelucci et al. (2024), we may therefore understand heightened government instability as a crucial catalyst for decreased voter turnout (the first, easier step of citizen political involvement), satisfaction with democracy and the government, and reduced political efficacy. In this sense, scholars have so far neglected to consider how instability affects essential elements of democratic quality, as illustrated by Diamond and Morlino (2004) and Morlino (2011).

Frequent government turnover and the legislature's inability to reach the full term stipulated by the constitution might be considered a major barrier to democratic norms and practices within the framework of democratic quality (Diamond & Morlino, 2004, p. 22). Furthermore, responsiveness – an additional aspect of democratic quality – may be impacted by unstable governments. In fact, responsiveness is interpreted by Diamond and Morlino (2004) as being closely related to "vertical accountability," and consequently to competition and participation. Accordingly, responsiveness influences the extent "to which citizens will be satisfied with the performance of democracy and view it as legitimate" (Diamond & Morlino, 2004, p. 28). Most importantly, according to Powell (2004, p. 91), governments are deemed responsive if they are able to "make and implement policies that citizens want." On the other hand, a government failing to survive in office faces several difficulties: governments in democratic systems seek to increase their reelection prospects. Therefore, they could make irresponsible use of public resources, manipulating the political business cycle (Nordhaus, 1975). Governments that are unstable fall short in formulating and implementing effective policies, failing to "deliver." Overall, the quality of democracy is severely harmed by government instability: high levels of instability should thus be seen as a democratic problem in Italy (and in those countries affected by short government duration and ensuing governmental performance issues).

2 Perspectives on government instability

Government instability has long been a central concern for political science, particularly within the framework of democratic theory. The recurring collapse of governments, especially in parliamentary systems, is often viewed as a sign of systemic issues that affect democratic performance and governance. In this section, I examine the broader theoretical debates regarding the functioning of democratic institutions in relation to the issue of government instability.

Democratic systems are fundamentally built on the idea that a certain amount of predictability is good for them (e.g., Chiaramonte & Emanuele, 2022). Predictability of party interactions, especially ruling parties, is an essential condition for effective decision-making. However, that can be highly influenced by the institutional design of a democracy, as discussed by Lijphart (1999). In majoritarian systems like the United Kingdom, government instability tends to arise from intra-party dynamics and leadership conflicts rather than from the structural deficits of coalition management. In consensual democracies, like Israel, government instability is often a direct result of the institutional framework that makes coalition government formation easier. In Italy, the constant need to manage diverging party interests, coupled with electoral systems encouraging fragmentation, usually lead to frequent cabinet turnover and, ultimately, a lack of policy continuity.

While Lijphart (1999) stressed the role of institutions, other scholars have focused on the actions and motivations of political actors when it comes to government instability (e.g., Sartori, 1976).

Adopting a more "behavioral" focus, we can stress the role of political actors' motivations, rather than institutions, particularly that of party leaders and members of parliament. Decisions made by political elites can either contribute to or mitigate government instability. For instance, the use of "blackmail potential" by junior coalition partners, as Sartori (1976) famously described, can significantly destabilize a government by creating internal pressures that lead to its premature end. In Italy, this dynamic has been particularly evident in the frequent withdrawals of support by junior coalition partners, such as the League and Italia Viva (Italy Alive), which led to the downfall of the Conte I and Conte II governments, respectively.

3 Empirical approach

This book examines the problem of government instability in Italy from different perspectives. To fully grasp the essence of this issue, it is necessary to look at it in the round, starting from its historical roots. Italy has indeed had a story of complex nation-building (e.g., Mack Smith, 1988), which has elicited poor social cohesion and limited trust in national institutions. Then, as I will argue in this book, the constitutional architecture of the country facilitated the emergence of conflict-ridden and short-lived cabinets. Therefore, to detect potential factors underpinning this phenomenon, the book studies government instability by considering the preferences of the drafters of the Italian constitution during the institution and rules' design period.

Moreover, to offer a comprehensive outlook of government instability in Italy and following Sartori's (1991) interpretation of comparative analysis work – in which he concluded that to understand a political system thoroughly, we need to put it in comparative perspective – the book compares the Italian case with other democracies over a period spanning from 1945 to today. Such a comparative outlook helps verify whether Italy is really an outlier or shares similarities with other political systems. Additionally, it helps identify the existence of different types of instability, going beyond government duration record.

Then, the empirical approach adopted in this book comprises the scrutiny of government instability and the concept of "policymaking accountability," which I measure here as the ruling parties' ability to be the protagonists of the whole policy cycle. In other words, ruling parties should be fully accountable if they are both the initiators and terminators of policy proposals. Such an examination helps investigate the effect of cabinet turnover on the policy cycle, as citizens may encounter difficulties attributing responsibility to specific government actors if the proponents and initiators of a specific policy differ from those implementing it.

Another objective of this book is to empirically assess the drivers of government instability in Italy by performing a Cox survival analysis. In detail, Cox analysis is a type of event-history analysis (Blossfeld et al., 2019) representing the standard in political science research on government stability (King et al., 1990). Initially, survival analysis was used to study issues in medical research. When performing quantitative investigations on the drivers of government stability, it is necessary to test whether the explanatory factors' effect is analyzed on the most informative types of terminations, namely discretionary ones. Indeed, not all cabinet terminations are equally important and signal instability and vulnerability. For example, governments may collapse simply because of regular elections, or even for causes related to the death or illness of governing personnel, or other constitutional reasons (Damgaard, 2008, p. 308). Such types of termination are not scientifically interesting. This book thus examines discretionary terminations – signs of governments' survival difficulties. These types of termination usually include, for instance, early elections, voluntary enlargement of the coalition, cabinet defeat, intra-party conflict, and inter-party personal conflict (Damgaard, 2008). With this in mind, the survival analysis of Italian governments will reveal the factors leading to increased risk of discretionary termination, particularly in terms of party conflicts and general vulnerability of the system.

Finally, adopting a constitutional engineering perspective (Sartori, 1995a), the book provides possible institutional remedies – also borrowing from successful comparative cases – for the instability issue in Italy. In particular, it provides policy and reform recommendations to policymakers and all those interested in tackling this issue and involved in the country's political process.

Overall, the book adopts an empirical, multi-method approach from a comparative perspective. Using different methodologies, the goal is to detect the various specificities of the Italian case (by, for instance, delving deeper into the historical and institutional roots of instability) and the broader picture of the instability's determinants. In addition, an essential resource provided in this book is the original multilevel dataset employed for the quantitative analysis behind the scrutiny of the instability's drivers and potential remedies. Specifically, the dataset has three levels: country, legislature, and government. A government is the basic unit of analysis. The sample includes 720 cabinets and 421 legislatures in 21 countries in a timespan covering the first cabinets born after the end of World War II up to the more recent executives of the 2020s. Therefore, to put Italy in a comparative perspective, this book investigates almost 80 years of political developments in the electoral and governmental arena of 21 democracies. The presented strategy aligns with previous cross-national research on governments that has widely employed extensive datasets to investigate government stability and other issues related to the cabinet life cycle (Franklin & Mackie, 1984; Warwick, 1994; Strøm et al., 2008). The 21 countries under examination are all ascribable to Europe except Israel, which can, however, be considered a country sharing many political similarities with Italy – for instance, regarding government instability and political fragmentation (e.g., Neuberger, 2020). Concerning the temporal framework, the dataset's extensive configuration allows verification of government instability trajectories over essential moments in the history of Italy.

Based on Müller et al. (2008) and Shomer et al. (2023), I counted a change of government with the following circumstances:

–   Change in the person of the prime minister, that is, the head of the cabinet, regardless of the specific title the cabinet might have (e.g., chancellor, prime minister, state minister).
–   Change in the party composition of the government, altering its status.
–   General election (constitutionally mandated or elicited by early legislature dissolution).

In the dataset, a government starts on the date of its inauguration. For example, Italian governments' start dates are recorded at the *giuramento* stage, that is, when the prime minister and ministers officially take office. The end date of the government is the date of the formal resignation or, alternatively, the general election date, "whichever comes first" (Müller & Strøm, 2000, p. 11).

Regarding the methodological approach, this book employs a multi-method empirical approach to examine the issue of government instability in Italy. The analysis draws from both historical and comparative perspectives to assess the underlying factors contributing to short government duration and frequent cabinet turnover. Each chapter adopts a tailored methodological strategy, focusing on specific aspects of instability, from historical roots to empirical models that capture some dynamics.

In detail, Chapter 2 performs a historical analysis to trace the roots of government instability in Italy, with an emphasis on the nation-building process and the constitutional framework established in 1948. This historical analysis is complemented by a comparative lens, comparing the Italian case with other Western democracies, particularly those that share similar issues of fragmentation and government instability. Archival research and secondary sources provide the foundation for this chapter's historical narratives. Finally, a qualitative analysis of the Italian constitution is performed.

Chapter 3 places Italy in a comparative perspective, examining government stability trajectories in other countries. In Chapter 4, the initiators and terminators of policy proposals are examined to highlight how the policy cycle is affected by cabinet turnover.

The book embarks on a more quantitative approach in Chapter 5. Specifically, I utilize Cox proportional hazards models to estimate the survival of Italian governments. This methodology, widely employed in medical research for studying the survival rates of medical patients, allows for an examination of the factors that increase the risk of early termination. The analysis time considered is government duration measured in days, with discretionary termination events coded as failure variables. The survival analysis allows one to estimate the impact of various covariates on the likelihood of a government's early termination. The Cox model is the preferred choice for studying government instability for the following reasons. First, it does not require assumptions about the shape of the baseline hazard function (i.e., how the risk of government collapse changes over time). This flexibility is crucial when analyzing political systems where the risk of government termination may vary unpredictably. Second, the Cox model accounts for right-censoring, which occurs when a government is still in office at the end of the study period or during data collection. This is relevant when scrutinizing government stability, where some governments may not yet have collapsed by the time the analysis is conducted. Third, the dynamic perspective ingrained in the Cox model makes it easier to incorporate time-varying covariates, allowing for the analysis of factors influencing the life cycle of a government.

The empirical analyses presented in this book rely on an original, multilevel dataset covering 21 democracies from 1945 to the present. The dataset includes more than 700 governments and 400 legislatures, with Italy serving as the focal case.[2] The basic unit of analysis is the government. Overall, the dataset spans almost 80 years of political developments in the region, allowing for the analysis of trends in government stability over time (Chapter 3). The inclusion of multiple countries enables the identification of broader patterns while contextualizing Italy. In particular, the dataset tracks the transition from the First to the Second and the Second to the Third Republic, providing a rich longitudinal perspective on Italian government instability.

Finally, considering the empirical approach, Chapter 6 adopts a constitutional engineering perspective, using comparative institutional analysis to propose reforms aimed at reducing government instability in Italy. Drawing from successful cases in countries like Germany and Spain, where institutional mechanisms such as constructive votes of no confidence and higher electoral thresholds have been useful in alleviating instability of governments, this chapter provides policy recommendations devoted to the Italian case – such suggestions might be considered from Italian policymakers, also considering that we are currently witnessing a season of institutional reforms (Improta & Marzi, 2024). The analysis concludes by including simulations of hypothetical reforms and their potential effects on government stability.

---

2 I started the data collection effort in 2017, when I was a Ph.D. Student at LUISS in Rome.

Chapter 2
A past still present: At the roots of government instability

This chapter scrutinizes the historical roots underpinning government instability in Italy. In particular, it emphasizes the poor social cohesion engendered by a troublesome country unification process whose consequences can still be traced in contemporary Italy. Additionally, the chapter underlines the role of constitutional architecture in facilitating the formation of conflict-ridden and short-lived cabinets in Italy.

1 A nation-less state?

Italy is only a geographic expression.
Count Klemens von Metternich, Chancellor of the Austrian Empire, 1814[3]

The consideration that Italy underwent a troubled process of unification is supported by many historians (e.g., Mack Smith, 1997). This is essentially due to the deep divisions that characterized the pre-unification period and the years immediately following the year of Italian unification, 1861. The Kingdom of Italy was born following a process of unification led by one of the kingdoms inhabiting the peninsula in the pre-unification phase, the Kingdom of Sardinia, which was ruled by Piedmont sovereigns culturally linked to France. It is therefore not surprising that the constitutional framework of the Kingdom of Italy was that of the Kingdom of Sardinia, the so-called "Albertine Statute" enacted in 1848. The statute of 1848 remained the fundamental charter upon which the Italian social pact was based for a long time, precisely until January 1, 1948, when the constitution of the Italian Republic came into force (Adams & Barile, 1953). The Albertine constitution, however, differed from the republican one. First, it was a flexible constitution. This is why its initial liberal framework was easily transformed into an authoritarian direction by fascism. Italian governmental instability, despite differences in constitutional provisions, was nonetheless evident even in the Albertine constitution. According to Mack Smith (1997, p. 39), an element of instability was apparent in the constitutional architecture of the Albertine Constitution: since collective responsibility of

---

3 The precise date of this statement is uncertain. Some sources suggest that it may have been written and uttered for the first time in 1847.

https://doi.org/10.1515/9783111329727-003

the cabinet was not considered essential, individual ministers had to preserve their tenure by defending their actions, irrespective of those of the entire government. This constituted a significant source of government instability, "so much so that in the period from 1861 to 1896, within 35 years, there were 33 governments" (Mack Smith, 1997, p. 39). In Mack Smith's view, the process of Italian national unification was essentially a civil war between the old and new ruling classes, particularly between those of the North and South of the peninsula. Regarding the masses, especially the peasants, there was no attachment for Italian unification. The unification process touched Southern populations in a different way, with higher economic costs felt in an increase in prices and taxes. Then, when the arrival of compulsory conscription became evident, citizens of the South started to have their first experiences with the new political entity.

Before 1861, Italy had not formed a political entity, and, as previously mentioned, even after that date, a common national sentiment had not developed in all areas of the country. As argued by Luigi Blanch, the patriotism of Italians was analogous to that of ancient Greeks, meaning it was "love for a single city rather than for a country; it was a tribal sentiment rather than a national one" (quoted in Mack Smith, 1997, p. 8). Only after foreign conquests did the "Italians" unite, but once the foreign danger was averted, they returned to division and a fragmented dynamic. Italy was politically divided in a very clear manner: Austrian domination reigned in Lombardy, Venice, and Tuscany, while Spanish rule held sway in Naples. Additionally, Piedmont controlled Genoa and Savoy but had strong French cultural influences. The Italian peninsula was inhabited by eight different states, each with its own currency, tariffs, and duties. Trade, which could have stimulated human exchange as well, was therefore highly hindered by these barriers. According to some historians (e.g., Zamagni, 1993), a timid, initial sense of Italian national sentiment began to mature under the influence of a widespread middle class in the Northern areas. However, this national sentiment stemmed from strictly market-related motivations; there was indeed a growing awareness of the importance of trade and commercial interactions for development in international relations. It is not coincidental that it was a nobleman in Piedmont with a focus on economics, Cavour, who initiated the process of national unification (Mack Smith, 1997).

The idea of creating the Italian nation was a subject of discussion that animated debate not only among the economic elites but also among the cultural elites (which often overlapped each other). Specifically, in the literary circles of the pre-unification states (particularly in Tuscany and Lombardy), the first literary works were born that formed the basis of Italian culture for centuries to come (notably Alessandro Manzoni's 1825 work, *I Promessi Sposi*). Literature, in this way, contributed to the development of a national consciousness (Körner, 2009). However, these efforts were confined to specific territories of the peninsula, certainly not to a cultural vibrancy that bound all cities in a sense of unity.

While the Kingdom of Italy was established in 1861, the construction of a unified national identity was far in the future. The lack of a common, shared national sentiment was evident. This situation started to change during the aftermath of World War II, which marked a critical period in the development of Italian national sentiment, particularly as the country transitioned from a monarchy to a republic and grappled with the consequences of fascism, occupation, and civil war (Clark, 2013). The formation of a national identity in post-war Italy was influenced by various factors, including the activity of political formations, the Catholic Church, and resistance movements, all of which played pivotal roles in shaping the collective sentiment of Italians (Riall, 2002).

As unification was a contested process that did not result in a strong national identity, the fascist regime under Mussolini attempted to forge a cohesive identity through the promotion of a new form of nationalism characterized by several symbols deriving from imperial Rome (Gentile, 2013). This identity was therefore closely tied to the regime's authoritarian and militaristic values. The fall of fascism and the subsequent experience of war and occupation altered the establishment of such values (Wanrooij, 1987).

In the immediate post-war period, Italy faced the challenge of reconstructing not only its economy and infrastructure but also its national identity. The 1946 referendum, which led to the establishment of the republic, was a significant turning point. This transition required a redefinition of what it meant to be Italian, as the new republic sought to distance itself from the fascist past and establish a democratic foundation (Pombeni, 2016). This objective was highly pursued by political parties. They played a crucial role in the construction of national sentiment in post-war Italy. The DC emerged as the dominant party, advocating for a moderate, centrist approach to reconcile the population after the civil war. The DC emphasized Catholic values, which were shared by several segments of Italian society, particularly in rural areas where the Church had a strong influence (Diamanti, 2009). The Partito Comunista Italiano (PCI) also played a significant role in shaping national identity. The PCI's roots in the antifascist resistance gave it considerable moral authority in the post-war years. The party emphasized social justice, workers' rights, and anti-imperialism, appealing to the industrial working class in the North and contributing to the development of a class-based aspect of national identity (Sani, 1973). The competition between the DC and the PCI was not just a political struggle but also a contest over the definition of Italian identity. The DC's vision of Italy was rooted in Catholicism, traditional family values, and a commitment to the West, while the PCI envisioned a more egalitarian society aligned with the socialist bloc. Despite these differences, both parties contributed to the formation of a democratic culture in Italy (Cotta & Verzichelli, 2007).

When reflecting on Italy as a nation-less state, we should consider the role of the Catholic Church. Italy's historical relationship with the Church had always been complex, given the Church's opposition to the unification of Italy in the 19th century. However, in the post-war period, the Church emerged as a stabilizing force, particularly through its support for the DC. The Church's role in education and social services allowed it to maintain a significant presence in Italian society, especially in rural areas. The Church's influence on national identity was also evident in its opposition to communism, which was interpreted as an existential threat to religious values. The Church's anti-communist stance contributed to polarizing Italian society during the Cold War, but it also reinforced the association between Catholicism and Italian identity for many segments of the population (Santagata, 2014).

Moreover, an important role in shaping Italian national identity was exerted by the memory of anti-fascist resistance. The resistance was not only a military struggle against the occupying Nazi forces and the fascist regime but also a broader social and political movement that sought to lay the foundations for a new, democratic Italy. The resistance provided a powerful narrative of national unity, which was used by political actors to legitimize their vision of the novel Italy (Pombeni, 2016). For the PCI, the resistance was a symbol of the working-class struggle against fascism, while for the DC it was related to spiritual strength. The commemoration of the resistance became a central feature of Italian public life, with annual celebrations of Liberation Day on April 25. These commemorations served to reinforce the democratic values that had emerged from the resistance and to form a sense of continuity between the anti-fascist struggle and the new republican order. However, the memory of the resistance was also a source of division. The civil war aspect of the resistance, in which Italians fought on both sides, left a legacy of mistrust that complicated the construction of a unified national identity. The tension between the desire to honor the struggle and the need to reconcile with former fascists and their sympathizers was a delicate balancing act for the post-war Italian state (Ignazi, 1989).

Despite the efforts to create a common national identity, regionalism (which has its roots in the difficult unification process described before) remained critical. The economic disparities between the industrialized North and the agrarian South persisted and even deepened in the post-war period. These regional differences were not only economic but also cultural and political, with the north generally more secular and the south more religious. The new state tried to address such disparities through several economic and social reforms, including the reform establishing the "Cassa per il Mezzogiorno" (Fund for the South), which aimed to stimulate economic development in the south. However, these efforts were only partially successful, and regional differences continued to coexist with the weak national identity. The persistence of regionalism also had political implications. The rise of regionalist and autonomous movements, such as the Northern League (Lega Nord) in the late 20th century, challenged the centralizing tendencies of the Italian state and called into question the very idea of a unified nation. These movements often framed their demands in terms of economic development, but they also tapped into deeper cultural and historical differences between the regions (e.g., Tarchi, 1998).

National identity is not a matter concerning politics and institutions only. In Italy, the media and popular culture exerted a relevant influence in the creation of a national sentiment. The expansion of television, particularly through the state broadcaster Radiotelevisione Italiana, made Italian culture popular. Radiotelevisione Italiana's programming, which included news, educational programs, and entertainment, helped to create a shared cultural experience for Italians, regardless of their regional or social background (a counterculture was eventually introduced by Berlusconi's Mediaset; see, for instance, De Angelis & Vecchiato, 2024). The media also played a role in shaping the memory of the recent past, including the fascist era and the resistance. Films, literature, and television programs often depicted the struggle against fascism and the hardships of the war, contributing to the formation of a collective memory that reinforced the values of democracy and anti-fascism (Penati, 2015). However, the media also reflected and sometimes reinforced regional differences. Local newspapers and radio stations catered to regional audiences, often emphasizing local issues and perspectives (e.g., Radio Padania). Moreover, the rise of commercial television in the 1980s, with its focus on entertainment and consumerism, contributed to the fragmentation of the national cultural space and the decline of traditional forms of national identity. Silvio Berlusconi, former prime minister and entrepreneur of private sector media, was the main actor driving this process (Ginsborg, 2005; De Angelis & Vecchiato, 2024).

The construction of national identity and sentiment in Italy was a complex and multifaceted process, shaped by several factors. The difficult unification process, the transition from monarchy to republic, the influence of different political cultures, the role of the Church, the memory of the resistance, and regionalism were fundamental in influencing trajectories of national identity formation and development. The legacy of the unification process and fascism, the challenges of economic reconstruction, and the regional disparities that continued to plague the country all contributed to a sense of ambivalence about the idea of a unified Italian nation. Currently, the tensions between national unity and regional diversity, between tradition and modernity, and between democracy and authoritarianism continue to limit the establishment of a shared sentiment of unity, which is still failing to emerge.

2 Constitutional design: Fearing excessive government power

Italy was under fascist rule for a period of around two decades (*ventennio fascista*), led by Benito Mussolini. Following the conclusion of World War II, Italy moved away from fascism and opted for a different form of governance. The experience of fascism under Mussolini had a profound impact on Italian politics. Mussolini's regime, which came to power in 1922, systematically dismantled democratic institutions, concentrated power in the hands of the executive, and suppressed political opposition. The fascist state's control over the media, education, and the economy, combined with its use of propaganda, created a climate of fear and conformity that stifled political dissent. The fall of Mussolini in 1943 and the subsequent liberation of Italy by Allied forces led to a period of intense political upheavals. The question of how to rebuild Italy was a pressing one, and it was clear that any new political system would have to address the abuses of the fascist period. The result was a constitution that sought to prevent the concentration of power.

In 1946, the Italians voted to shift from a monarchy to a republic. This decision needed the creation of a new constitutional framework for the newly formed Italian republic, a process that involved extensive deliberations and discussions among the diverse political factions represented in the constituent assembly in December 1947. The constitution officially took effect on January 1, 1948. Many scholars view the Italian constitution as a product of negotiations and compromises among various political ideologies, including communists, Christian democrats, secularists, and liberals.

The constituent assembly was elected by universal suffrage on June 2, 1946. The composition of the newly elected assembly was essentially represented by three main forces. On one side, the DC, of Catholic inspiration, and on the other, the left-wing parties: the Italian Socialist Party (PSI) and the PCI. The liberal component was marginal, having gathered fewer votes at the polls. The two main ideological features were indeed the social doctrine of the Church and the socialist and communist imprint. These two souls gave life to the work on the constitution, with liberal parties playing a more peripheral role in legislative drafting. According to Martelli (2018), the liberals were not able to influence the decisions of the constituent assembly regarding the political culture expressed in the constitution.

As mentioned previously, the Italian constituents drafted the constitution after World War II. Therefore, they had in mind the authoritarian experience of the past while discussing the possible constitutional provisions to be included in building the new institutional framework of the country. This phenomenon was described as "tyrant syndrome," namely the fear felt by the Italian founding fathers about the return of dictatorship. For this reason, the objective of the constituent assembly was to limit the government's margins of maneuver as much as possible. However, although this objective was understandable given the historical moment within which it was situated, it laid the groundwork for governance performance issues that still plague Italian governments today. Indeed, despite some exceptions (e.g., Partito d'Azione), the drafters of the Italian constitution sought to avoid excessive executive power, preferring, for instance, consensus-oriented institutional provisions rather than majoritarian solutions (Pombeni, 2016). All this indicated the fear of ceding excessive power to a political system's governmental branch.

How has the instability of governments been influenced by the measures inserted in the constitution in 1948? Could tyrant syndrome have excessively weakened the power of Italian governments to impose their own political agenda and improve their performance capacity? Which elements have provided a fertile ground for the emergence of unstable governments throughout the life of the Italian Republic? To answer these questions, a detailed analysis of the Italian constitution is required.

The constitution is composed of 139 articles and 18 transitional and final provisions. As mentioned above, it represents a text written and approved in the postwar period, and takes on the characteristic of a "rigid" constitution, meaning it is difficult to amend subsequently, as numerous failed reform attempts have demonstrated (Baldini, 2017; D'Alimonte & Mammarella, 2022; Improta & Marzi, 2024). As noted by Martelli (2018, p. 5), the Italian constitution is often referred to as "the most beautiful in the world," probably a reflection its stylistic and literary characteristics rather than its effectiveness.

The main architect of the Italian constitution was the DC. In those years, the secretary of the DC was Alcide De Gasperi, a moderate representative of this political faction. The goal was to overcome the fascist experience by laying the groundwork for its non-recurrence. But the objective was not limited to this. There was also the idea that the liberal model preceding the establishment of fascism was excessively risky, as it had allowed fascism to emerge. In this endeavor, De Gasperi could count on the collaboration of a pragmatic communist secretary: Palmiro Togliatti of the PCI. In this way, the PCI and DC collaborated on various fronts: from the theme of the state–Church relationship in the constitution to social and economic relations, which were to be distant from the liberal perspective. In this manner, the constitution took on a character dominated by the presence of explicit references to moral values, which went beyond mere references to individual rights as desired by the liberals.

Moving to the constitutional issue regarding the government, what role was envisioned for the government by the constituent assembly? A marginal role. The constitution lacks indications about the role of the government in the new Italian state. As highlighted by Martelli (2018), government is mentioned in the section on the formation of laws primarily to limit its legislative function, while the council of ministers is allotted only five articles, from Article 92 to Article 96, totaling 248 words. The part of the constitution dedicated to the government is Third Title, Section I: The Council of Ministers.

The articles are the following:
–   Art. 92: The Government of the Republic is made up of the President of the Council and the Ministers who together form the Council of Ministers. The President of the Republic appoints the President of the Council of Ministers and, on his proposal, the Ministers.
–   Art. 93: Before taking office, the President of the Council of Ministers and the Ministers shall be sworn in by the President of the Republic.
–   Art. 94: The Government must receive the confidence of both Houses of Parliament. Each House grants or withdraws its confidence through a reasoned motion voted on by roll-call. Within ten days of its formation the Government shall come before Parliament to obtain confidence. An opposing vote by one or both the Houses against a Government proposal does not entail the obligation to resign. A motion of no confidence must be signed by at least one-tenth of the members of the House and cannot be debated earlier than three days from its presentation.
–   Art. 95: The President of the Council conducts and holds responsibility for the general policy of the Government. The President of the Council ensures the coherence of political and administrative policies, by promoting and coordinating the activity of the Ministers. The Ministers are collectively responsible for the acts of the Council of Ministers; they are individually responsible for the acts of their own ministries. The law establishes the organization of the Presidency of the Council, as well as the number, competence, and organization of the ministries.

- Art. 96: The President of the Council of Ministers and the Ministers, even if they resign from office, are subject to normal justice for crimes committed in the exercise of their duties, provided authorization is given by the Senate of the Republic or the Chamber of Deputies, in accordance with the norms established by Constitutional Law.

Such articles primarily address procedural matters such as appointment, confidence vote, government responsibility, and the impeachment of ministers. Article 95 pays attention to a generic description of the political and administrative coordination role of the prime minister, positioning the prime minister as a *primus inter pares* among other cabinet members. The government thus received remarkably little attention from the drafters of the constitution. This is not the case for other institutions, such as the parliament and the presidency of the republic. The parliament receives greater attention: 28 articles (from 55 to 82) amounting to a total of 1436 words (Martelli, 2018). For the president of the republic, there are 9 articles (from 83 to 91) totaling 551 words (Martelli, 2018). Additionally, as Martelli (2018, p. 42) points out, there is an even greater focus on the National Council for Economics and Labor – an auxiliary and less significant body – compared with the government.

The constitution also includes provisions for the dissolution of parliament and the calling of new elections, but these powers are carefully circumscribed to prevent abuse. The president of the Republic could dissolve parliament, but only after consulting both chambers.

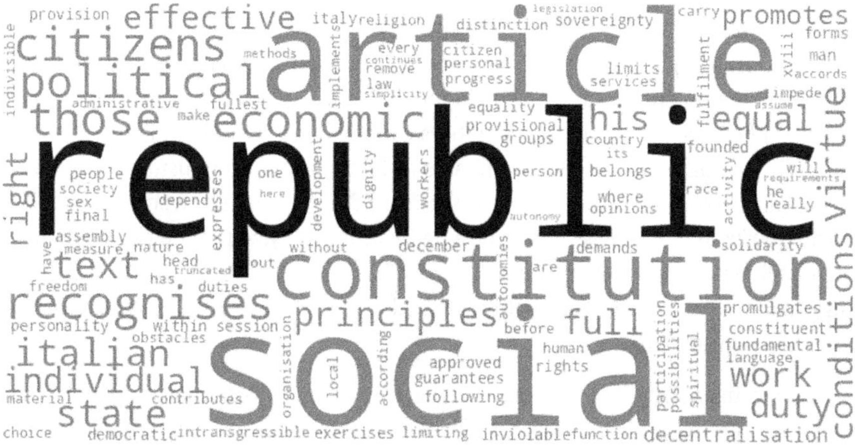

Figure 2.1: Word cloud of the Italian constitution (English version).
Source: Own elaboration.

As documented in Figure 2.1, the constitution lacks clear references to the role of the government, and the need to ensure the stability of this body was only referenced in parliamentary debates, which, however, did not impact the constitution's final draft. All this is combined with a clear desire to follow a consensual democratic model (Lijphart, 1999) and proportional approach regarding the electoral system. A proportional electoral system, in fact, ensured that all political cultures were represented in parliament. This perspective, which was maintained until the collapse of the so-called First Republic in 1992, has, as we will see in the following chapters, led to evident government instability. Some members of the constituent assembly had foreseen the possible degeneration of the parliamentary system, however. For example, in his report presented to the 1946 constitutional commission, Costantino Mortati – a constitutional law expert – had raised the issue of government instability. Specifically, Mortati highlighted the need to ensure the government's stability of political direction to avoid a hectic turnover of governments and lack of unity and continuity in their work. This elicited a debate on which form of government was preferable: parliamentarism or presidentialism. There were different stances, but those inclined towards the parliamentary form were predominant. However, some of the potential problems of parliamentarism had already been identified. According to many constituents, it was clear that the country would be heading towards a form that would likely generate instability and limited effectiveness of governments. Tyrant syndrome was at the root of the preference for parliamentarism. But it was not the only reason. Piero Calamandrei pointed out in his intervention in September 1946 that a weak democracy is a democracy with many governments with a short time horizon, rather than a democracy that entrusts many powers to the head of government. Another element of instability lies in the redundant bicameral system (see Article 94) desired by the drafters. This represents a further Italian peculiarity. Indeed, the government needs to obtain confidence in both chambers, on two different occasions. A confidence withdrawal in one of the chambers can give rise to a government crisis – a situation that often occurred in all phases of Italian republican history. This is one of the most significant ways in which the fear of government power emerged. The Italian parliament was designed to be a deliberative body, with both chambers having equal powers in the legislative process. This bicameralism was intended to ensure that laws would be thoroughly debated and scrutinized, reducing the risk of hasty decision-making.

Moreover, instability can be traced in the motion of no confidence. As noted recently by Lento and Hazan (2023), there are different types of no-confidence votes that make it easier or harder to trigger a government crisis by the parliament and lead to the fall of a government. Unlike Germany and Spain, the Italian constitution has opted for a simple vote of no confidence, which thus requires a majority of members of the chambers to bring down a government. To ensure greater stability, the drafters could have included a vote of constructive no confidence, which would make it more difficult to end a government because parliamentarians must identify a substitute prime minister ready to take over from the one being voted out, thereby creating an element of accountability for the legislative branch. Evidently, providing the executive with this protective instrument in the historical period in which the constitution was written could have seemed excessively favorable to the government, which instead needed to be as controllable as possible by the legislative branch.

Although the constitution did not include any reference to the need to ensure government stability, there were divisions in the debates regarding the choice of the form of government. From this perspective, some constituents like Giorgio Amendola of the PCI believed that the stability of governments was not related to the form of government but to the level of "political consciousness" of the parties and the party system. Specifically, Amendola argued as follows: "Today discipline, stability is given by political consciousness, entrusted to the action of political parties."[4]

The lack of political consciousness that was observed in the years to come effectively led Italy to have unstable governments, as many of the causes of government collapse over the decades were related to internal conflicts within a coalition. The drafters overwhelmingly approved the option of parliamentarism and attempts by some constitutionalists to include elements of rationalization of parliamentarism failed.

Moreover, the constitution established the Constitutional Court, a body tasked with ensuring that laws and government actions were in compliance with the constitution. The Constitutional Court was given the power to review the constitutionality of laws, strike down those that violated constitutional principles, and resolve conflicts between different branches of government. This judicial oversight was seen as a crucial mechanism for preventing the concentration of power and protecting individual rights.

Another key feature of the Italian constitution was its emphasis on decentralization and regional autonomy. The framers of the constitution were keenly aware of the dangers of centralization, having witnessed how the fascist regime had concentrated power and imposed its authority on the local level. To counteract this,

---

4 G. Amendola, *Atti Ass. Cost. Seconda sottocommissione*, 1946, p. 124–125.

the constitution established a system of regional governments in the 1970s, with some delegated functions in areas such as education, health, and infrastructure. The establishment of regions was not only a response to the fascist era but also an acknowledgment of Italy's historical regional diversity. The constitution recognized that a one-size-fits-all approach to governance was not appropriate for a country with such varied economic and social conditions. By granting regions a degree of autonomy, the constitution created a more flexible system that could better meet the needs of different parts of the country. However, the flipside of this choice was to further increase the fragmentation and transaction costs of decision-making processes. The decentralization of power, indeed, was also extended to local governments, with municipalities and provinces given considerable responsibilities for local administration. This multi-tiered system of government was designed to prevent excessive government power, but eventually gave rise to constrained political administrations (mostly at the national level).

The fear of excessive government power in the Italian constitution was also shaped by the influence of international models. The framers of the constitution drew on a range of experiences from other countries, particularly those that had successfully established stable democratic systems after periods of authoritarian rule. The Italian constitution was influenced by the Weimar constitution of Germany, which had sought to create a democratic order after World War I but had ultimately failed to prevent the rise of Nazism. The drafters of the Italian constitution were aware of the weaknesses of the Weimar system, particularly its lack of effective checks on executive power, and tried to avoid similar pitfalls in Italy. However, they opted for a consensual model of democracy adopted by the Weimar Republic, which can exacerbate conflicts among different population strata and associated political formations. This eventually led to short government duration in both experiences. Moreover, the Italian constitution was also influenced by the French and British systems, especially in terms of the separation of powers, but the Italian system was unique in its emphasis on proportional representation and the role of political parties, reflecting the specific challenges and concerns of the Italian context of the time.

All in all, the Italian constitution of 1948 was characterized by a profound fear of excessive government power, born out of the experience of fascism and the desire to establish a stable, enduring democratic system. This fear influenced every aspect of the constitution, particularly the structure and functions of the government and the decentralization of the state. The final result was a constitution that prevented power concentration, which in turn elicited frequent government collapses.

Chapter 3
Italy in a longitudinal and comparative perspective

To offer a comprehensive look at government instability in Italy, this chapter puts the Italian case in a longitudinal and comparative perspective by providing a picture of the patterns and dynamics of government instability in other European countries. It highlights the existence of different types of instability: from frenetic cabinet turnover and short government duration to low party returnability and ministerial experience in office.

1 Temporal and spatial trends

The instability of Italian governments is a defining feature of the country's political system, recognized both domestically and internationally. The short duration of governments in Italy has characterized the political landscape since the establishment of the Republic in 1948. As discussed previously, this chronic instability is rooted in the constitutional architecture designed and approved by the drafters of the constitution, which, while aiming to prevent the resurgence of authoritarianism, also created a highly fragmented and consensus-driven political environment.

Starting from 1948, Italian governments have struggled to achieve the levels of stability observed in other Western European democracies, placing Italy among the most unstable political systems in Europe (King et al., 1990; Cotta & Marangoni, 2015; Curini & Pinto, 2017;Improta, 2023). However, this instability is far from uniform and has evolved over time. As noted by Mershon (1996), during the period from 1948 to 1992, the era of the First Republic, governments were typically short-lived, yet the political class remained remarkably consistent. This reflects a type of instability that affected the survival of individual cabinets but not the political personnel that occupied key ministerial positions. In this regard, the rapid turnover of governments masked a deeper continuity of political elites, with long-standing coalitions and alliances driving much of the policymaking process.

Similarly, Calise (2015) observed that governments formed after 1948, though characterized by short durations, exhibited high levels of continuity among the politicians and ministers holding key positions (see also Improta, 2022b; Fittipaldi & Musella, 2022). The same political actors often rotated between different government configurations, ensuring that despite frequent changes in cabinet com-

https://doi.org/10.1515/9783111329727-004

position, there was little change in the overall direction of governance. This phenomenon of ruling stability amid government instability (Improta, 2022b) became evident during the whole 1948–1992 phase.

During this period, Italy's governments were often coalitions of centrist parties, primarily dominated by the DC, which remained in power for the entire period. The average duration of a government was often less than a year, with many governments falling due to internal disagreements and coalition conflict. Despite this hectic turnover, the political elites at the core of these governments remained relatively unchanged. The DC, in particular, maintained a hegemonic position within the political system, ensuring that any government crisis or collapse would ultimately result in a new coalition led by the same political actors, with only minimal reshuffling of ministerial portfolios.

This pattern of political continuity amidst governmental change reflected the consensus-based nature (Lijphart, 1999) of Italian politics during the First Republic. The emphasis on broad coalition-building meant that governments were often precariously balanced coalitions of ideologically diverse parties. The early 1990s marked a significant turning point in Italian politics, as the *Tangentopoli* scandal and the subsequent *Mani Pulite* investigation led to the collapse of the traditional party system that had dominated the First Republic. The DC, along with several other major parties, disintegrated, paving the way for new political forces to emerge. This period, known as the transition to the Second Republic, was characterized by a shift from a proportional electoral system to a mixed system.

Figure 3.1 displays the average government duration across 21 countries from 1940 to the first part of the 21st century. The black line represents the changes in average government duration over time, while the red dashed line indicates the median duration. The initial period, from the 1940s to the early 1950s, is marked by significant volatility in government durations. This reflects the post-war political instability experienced in many countries, as new political orders and democratic institutions were being established in the aftermath of the war. Frequent changes of government during this period may be attributed to the transitional nature of political systems and the challenges of post-war reconstruction.

After that period, there is a timid stabilization in the average government duration. During this period, many Western democracies experienced an era of relative political stability, as post-war recovery consolidated and political institutions became more entrenched. Governments tended to endure longer than was the case during the immediate post-war years. However, renewed fluctuations in government duration can be observed in later periods. In particular, after the 2000s, the trend indicates increasing instability, with a sharp decline in the average du-

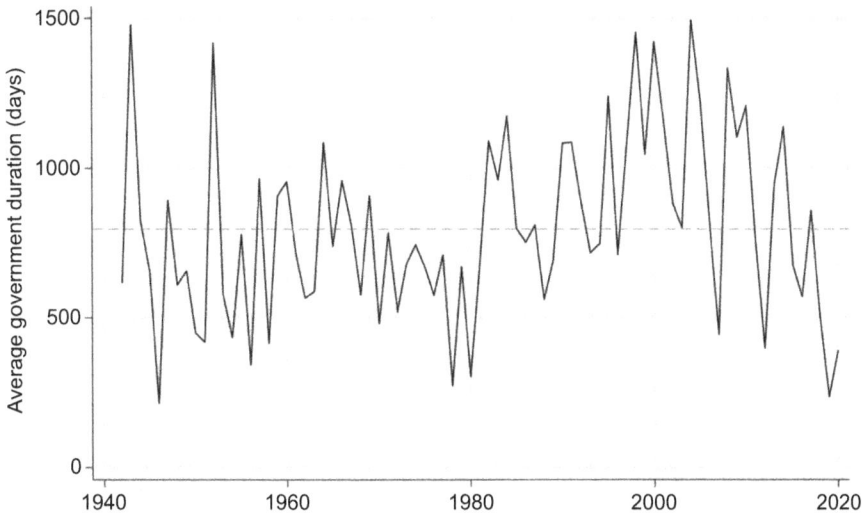

Figure 3.1: Average government duration per decade.
Source: Own elaboration.

ration of governments. This may be connected to the eruption of economic crises (e.g., the 2008 financial crisis), which have contributed to frequent government collapses in many democracies. Most importantly, the current period is characterized by the most critical instability European democracies have faced when it comes to government duration.

Figure 3.2 presents the average government duration across the sample of countries, comparing the length of time governments stay in power on average. Italy stands out as one of the political systems with a notably short average government duration. Compared with countries like Germany, Luxembourg, and Switzerland, which exhibit much higher average government durations, Italy's political system demonstrates chronic instability. At the other end of the spectrum, Belgium, Greece, and France also experience short average government durations. Belgium and Greece, like Italy, have problems with party conflicts (Belgium) and general vulnerability (Greece). Among the Mediterranean countries, Spain, Portugal, and Malta managed to achieve higher levels of stability. In particular, this latter country benefits from a majority-oriented bipartism which makes it easier to form single-party majority governments led by the Labour or by the Nationalist party, establishing patterns of alternation in the governmental arena.

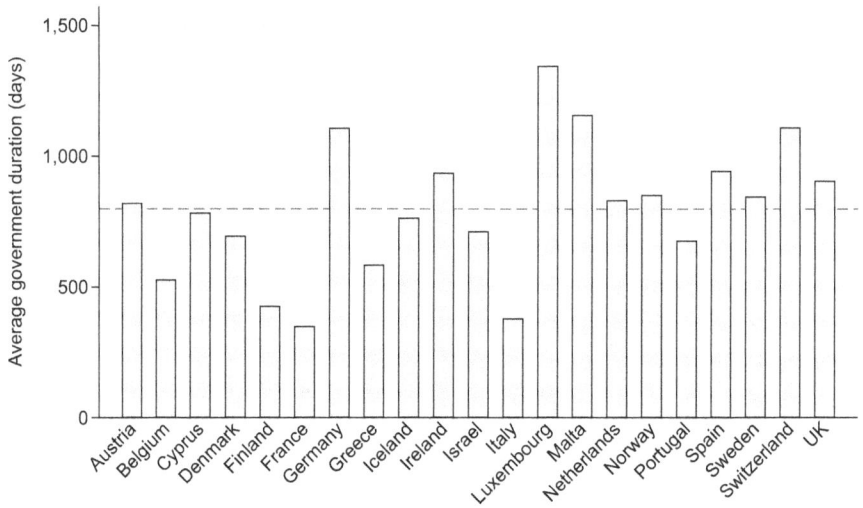

Figure 3.2: Average government duration per country.
Source: Own elaboration.

2 Types of instability

The duration of governments is not the only indicator of instability. Drawing on the distinction made by Battegazzorre (1987), it is necessary to delve into both government instability and ruling instability (see also Improta, 2022b). In this chapter, I attempt to identify the patterns of government duration and the level of innovation while also tracing the most frequent events that have led to the downfall of Italian governments from 1948 onwards. To this end, I study three possible macro categories, following past studies on the topic (e.g., Damgaard, 2008). First, I consider causes of downfall that stem from internal conflicts, both inter-party and intra-party. Second, I analyze the government's vulnerability to external shocks and critical events (Browne et al., 1984). Lastly, since governments can also fall peacefully, I also examine cases of technical downfall.

It is important to emphasize that not all types of downfall are equal, as different causes of government termination can indicate different issues. For example, a government that falls due to internal conflicts within the coalition signals a political and managerial problem within the coalition. A government that falls due to economic crises indicates issues in managing the macroeconomic cycle. Lastly, a government that falls because of new elections does not signal any problem, as this is a peaceful and natural end to its life cycle.

Following the approaches of the structural attributes school (Strøm et al., 2008) and critical events (Browne et al., 1984), I consider inter-party and intra-party conflicts concerning all cabinet terminations resulting from political or personal conflicts between coalition partners, as well as tensions between party factions (Damgaard, 2008). Such terminations can be seen as potential outcomes of the cabinet's structural attributes, such as having a surplus majority or high government fragmentation (Strøm et al., 2008). General vulnerability includes termination events related to social unrest, lack of party discipline in parliamentary votes, scandals, economic turmoil, and losses in second-order elections. These terminations are typical causes of cabinet collapse accentuated by event theorists (Browne et al., 1984), who highlight the impact of exogenous shocks on cabinet longevity, regardless of the coalition's structural features. Finally, technical reasons indicate cabinets that terminate because they failed to pass investiture votes or have reached the end of their term (Damgaard, 2008). Internal conflicts tend to be the primary sources of cabinet terminations in most fragmented governments in divided democracies (Lijphart, 1999). Echoing Lowell's famous "axiom of politics" (1896, p. 73), "the larger the number of discordant groups that form the majority, the harder the task of pleasing them all, and the more feeble and unstable the position of the cabinet" (see also Lijphart, 1984, p. 108).

To place Italy in a comparative perspective, I utilize an original, manually collected dataset containing information on approximately 700 governments across 21 European democracies starting from 1945. This way, we can understand the instability of Italian governments by looking at the situation in other political systems. However, we cannot fully grasp the characteristics of Italian government instability if we only analyze the duration of governments. As Battegazzorre (1987) notes, to study instability in Italy, we must also consider additional factors that can accompany the examination of government duration. In particular, political stability can persist even if the country experiences a frenetic turnover of governments, as was the case with the stable instability in Italy during the period 1948–1992 (Improta, 2022b). To follow Battegazzorre's suggestion, in this chapter I study not only the duration of governments but also additional factors.

To study the trajectories of instability in Italy, both in terms of government instability and ruling instability, it is necessary to consider a temporal differentiation. This is because the evolution of Italian political transformations cannot be fully understood without taking into account some historically significant breakpoints from a political perspective. In this chapter, I rely on a temporal differentiation that considers the evolution of the party system, as I have done in other past studies (e.g., Improta, 2022b). Specifically, the first phase spans from 1948 to 1994 and is the phase described by Sartori (1976) as "polarized multipartism." During this phase, the DC played a fundamental role (as a "pivot") in the party system, allying with smaller parties to ensure a parliamentary majority capable of keeping the so-called "anti-system" political formations on the periphery of the political space. The second phase began in 1994 and ended in 2013. It is a phase characterized by "fragmented bipolarism" (D'Alimonte, 2005), where there are two poles (center-right and center-left) contending for electoral victory. It represents a simplified political competition with hints of alternation dynamics, but still with a high level of fragmentation within the coalitions opposed to each other. The third and current phase, which began in 2013, has been interpreted, considering the de-institutionalized party system, as "volatile tripolarism" (Chiaramonte & Emanuele, 2013, 2022).

As shown in Table 3.1, the Italian party system, with its fluctuating actors, patterns, and rules, has been characterized for about three decades by numerous transformations that make it very complex to predict the country's political-electoral trajectories and the stability of the relationships between the forces that animate it. In particular, starting from 2013 the Italian party system went through a phase of great turbulence, producing effects both in terms of electoral stability and regarding the more general political stability of the country.

The next phase of turbulence, which begins immediately after the March 2018 elections and concludes with the new elections in September 2022, once again confirms the traditional formula of "continuous change and continuity in change" (Zucchini & Pedrazzani, 2021). The 2018 elections had delivered a historic result to the M5S: 32.7% of the vote. However, the center-right coalition (League, Brothers of Italy, Forza Italia) had reached 37%. Consequently, this situation had led to a hung parliament, characterized by the absence of a clear majority emerging from the polls. In this scenario, as has happened in the past, the pre-election coalitions dissolved, and each party went its own way. This gave rise to ideologically heterogeneous governments. The Conte I government was characterized, in terms of its political agenda, by some important decisions that would fuel public debate in the years to come. On the one hand, the League achieved a pension tax reform, and on the other hand, the M5S introduced a form of income support.

Despite these achievements, the traditional Italian government instability (Cotta & Verzichelli, 2007) persisted throughout the legislature, as shown in the table. After a little over a year in power, in fact, the first of the three government crises that characterized the legislature erupted. The crisis in August 2019 was based on leader of the League, Matteo Salvini's dissatisfaction with what he perceived as the coalition partner's inactivity. However, it also stemmed from the opportunity for the League to benefit from a growth in popularity at the expense of the M5S, as

Table 3.1: Italian governments since 1948.

Cabinet	Legislature	Cabinet duration (days)	Cabinet seat share (%)	Party composition	PM party	N. parties	N. ministers
De Gasperi IV	1948–1953	598	63	DC, PSDI, PLI, PRI	DC	4	21
De Gasperi V	1948–1953	534	61	DC, PSDI, PRI	DC	3	19
De Gasperi VI	1948–1953	704	54	DC, PRI	DC	2	18
De Gasperi VII	1953–1958	12	51	DC	DC	1	18
Pella	1953–1958	141	54	DC	DC	1	19
Fanfani	1953–1958	11	51	DC	DC	1	19
Scelba	1953–1958	497	50	DC, PSDI, PLI	DC	3	22
Segni	1953–1958	670	50	DC, PSDI, PLI	DC	3	21
Zoli	1953–1958	395	51	DC	DC	1	22
Fanfani II	1958–1963	208	50	DC, PSDI	DC	2	23
Segni II	1958–1963	373	57	DC	DC	1	23
Tambroni	1958–1963	115	50	DC	DC	1	24
Fanfani III	1958–1963	555	53	DC	DC	1	24
Fanfani IV	1958–1963	448	50	DC, PSDI, PRI	DC	3	24
Leone	1963–1968	136	41	DC	DC	1	24

(continued)

Table 3.1 (continued)

Cabinet	Legislature	Cabinet duration (days)	Cabinet seat share (%)	Party composition	PM party	N. parties	N. ministers
Moro	1963–1968	204	57	DC, PSI, PRI, PSDI	DC	4	28
Moro II	1963–1968	578	61	DC, PSI, PRI, PSDI	DC	4	26
Moro III	1963–1968	832	61	DC, PSI, PRI, PSDI	DC	4	26
Leone II	1968–1972	147	42	DC	DC	1	22
Rumor	1968–1972	204	58	DC, PSI, PSDI, PRI	DC	4	26
Rumor II	1968–1972	185	56	DC	DC	1	25
Rumor III	1968–1972	100	58	DC, PSI, PSDI, PRI	DC	4	27
Colombo	1968–1972	527	58	DC, PSI, PSDI, PRI	DC	4	27
Andreotti	1968–1972	8	42	DC	DC	1	26
Andreotti II	1972–1976	351	50	DC, PSDI, PLI	DC	3	27
Rumor IV	1972–1976	237	58	DC, PSI, PSDI, PRI	DC	4	29
Rumor V	1972–1976	202	58	DC, PSI, PSDI	DC	3	26
Moro IV	1972–1976	410	58	DC, PRI	DC	2	26
Moro V	1972–1976	78	42	DC	DC	1	22
Andreotti III	1976–1979	535	42	DC	DC	1	22

Andreotti IV	1976–1979	324	42	DC	DC	1	22
Andreotti V	1976–1979	10	46	DC, PSDI, PRI	DC	3	23
Cossiga	1979–1983	227	46	DC, PSDI, PLI	DC	3	25
Cossiga II	1979–1983	177	54	DC, PRI, PSI	DC	3	28
Forlani	1979–1983	220	57	DC, PSI, PRI, PSDI	DC	4	27
Spadolini	1979–1983	404	58	PRI, DC, PSI, PSDI, PLI	PRI	5	28
Spadolini II	1979–1983	82	59	PRI, DC, PSI, PSDI, PLI	PRI	5	28
Fanfani V	1979–1983	148	56	DC, PSI, PSDI, PLI	DC	4	28
Craxi	1983–1987	1058	58	PSI, DC, PRI, PSDI, PLI	PSI	5	30
Craxi II	1983–1987	214	58	PSI, DC, PRI, PSDI, PLI	PSI	5	30
Fanfani VI	1983–1987	11	35	DC	DC	1	27
Goria	1987–1992	226	59	DC, PSI, PRI, PSDI, PLI	DC	5	32
De Mita	1987–1992	401	59	DC, PSI, PRI, PSDI, PLI	DC	5	32
Andreotti VI	1987–1992	614	59	DC, PSI, PRI, PSDI, PLI	DC	5	33
Andreotti VII	1987–1992	377	56	DC, PSI, PSDI, PLI	DC	4	34
Amato	1992–1994	298	52	PSI, DC, PLI, PSDI	PSI	4	29
Ciampi	1992–1994	259	52	DC, PSI, PSDI, PLI	Independent	4	26
Berlusconi	1994–1996	225	55	FI, LN, AN, CCD	FI	4	27
Dini	1994–1996	359	48		Independent	Full technocratic	23

(continued)

Table 3.1 (continued)

Cabinet	Legislature	Cabinet duration (days)	Cabinet seat share (%)	Party composition	PM party	N. parties	N. ministers
Prodi	1996–2001	874	52	PPI, PDS, FDV, RI, UD	PPI	5	24
D'Alema	1996–2001	423	53	DS, PPI, FDV, RI, SDI, UDR, PDCI	PCI/PDS	7	28
D'Alema II	1996–2001	119	56,2	DS, PPI, RI, PDCI, VERDI, DEMO, UDEUR	PCI/PDS	7	27
Amato II	1996–2001	400	55	DS, PPI, RI, PDCI, FDV, DEMO, UDER, SDI	Independent	8	26
Berlusconi II	2001–2006	1409	56	FI, AN, LN, CCD, CDU	FI	5	25
Berlusconi III	2001–2006	374	54	FI, AN, LN, UDC, NPSI, PRI	FI	4	27
Prodi II	2006–2008	617	54	PDS, MARG, PRC, RNP, IDV, PDCI, FDV, UDEUR	ULIVO	8	28
Berlusconi IV	2008–2013	1283	54	PDL, LN	PDL	2	22
Monti	2008–2013	401	87		Independent	Full-technocratic	20
Letta	2013–2018	292	73	PD, PDL, SC, RADICALI, UDC	PD	5	22
Renzi	2013–2018	1019	59	PD, NCD, SC, UDC	PD	4	17
Gentiloni	2013–2018	467	54	PD, NCD, CPE	PD	3	19

Conte	2018–2022	460	53	M5S, LEGA	Independent	2	20
Conte II	2018–2022	526	55	M5S, PD, LEU	Independent	3	23
Draghi	2018–2022	617	88	M5S, LEGA, FDI, PD, FI, IV, MDP, +EU	Independent	8	24

Note: Pre-1948 De Gasperi cabinets and the current Meloni government are excluded; party composition is considered at the formation stage.
Source: Own elaboration, adaptation of Improta (2022b).

indicated by polls since the beginning of the legislative term. The ultimate outcome of this crisis, however, was a new mandate for Giuseppe Conte, who then became the leader of the M5S. Thus, the Conte II government was born, with a more progressive stance, with the parties of the center-right coalition in opposition.

The Conte II government was operating in an increasingly complex international environment. The global health crisis caused by the Covid-19 pandemic severely challenged every country in the world. Italy was the first European country to be affected. Conte was facing one of the most delicate emergency situations in the country's history with limited political experience behind him. The life of the Conte II government was beginning to falter in the early 2020s, and inter-party relations consequently experienced further transformations. Discontent within the governing coalition resulted in a second government crisis. Conte's attempts to seek an alternative majority in parliament failed.

Against this background of great instability, the option of a technocratic government re-emerged. Italy is known as a promised land of technocracy (Marangoni, 2012; Verzichelli & Cotta, 2018; Improta, 2021), and the last technocratic prime minister, as shown in the table, was Mario Draghi, former president of the European Central Bank. The Draghi government was born with well-defined goals. Front the pandemic, complete the vaccination campaign, manage the recovery plan. Draghi was sworn in in February 2021, and supporting him were many parties, but with the exception of Brothers of Italy, the party of the current prime minister Giorgia Meloni, and other political formations such as Nicola Fratoianni's Sinistra Italiana. The formation of the Draghi government was accompanied by a broad international consensus, based primarily on its credibility regarding compliance with supranational constraints and effectiveness in policymaking (Marangoni & Kreppel, 2022). It was also on this basis that the perceived political expediency of the parties that agreed to participate in the government had matured. In this sense, Draghi's credibility served as an important incentive for the governing parties to benefit from the possible success of the executive. Until January 2022, the heterogeneous coalition supporting Draghi coexisted peacefully, limiting conflicts. After a few months, however, the third government crisis of the legislature erupted.

Table 3.2 provides a detailed account of the reasons behind the termination of various Italian cabinets, spanning from the post-World War II era up to the Draghi government in 2022. It reveals the existence of recurring problems underpinning the collapse of Italian governments, highlighting both the complexity of some political dynamics and the ingrained difficulties in maintaining stable coalitions in a multiparty, fragmented political system like the Italian one.

Table 3.2: Causes of cabinet termination in Italy, 1948-today.

Cabinet	Legislature	Cause of termination	Description of termination event
De Gasperi IV	1948–1953	Inter-party conflicts	During the cabinet's tenure the PSDI decides to leave the coalition. Consequently, the cabinet voluntarily resigns to reconcile with the coalition partner
De Gasperi V	1948–1953	Intra-party conflicts	Troubles inside the PSDI and conflicts with the largest coalition party about social reforms
De Gasperi VI	1948–1953	General vulnerability	The senate approves downpayment bill for civil servants, in contrast to De Gasperi's agenda
De Gasperi VII	1953–1958	Technical reasons	The cabinet does not pass the investiture vote (lower chamber)
Pella	1953–1958	Intra-party conflicts	Resignation after a negative negotiation with the parliamentary groups of the DC
Fanfani	1953–1958	Technical reasons	The cabinet does not pass the investiture vote (lower chamber)
Scelba	1953–1958	Intra-party conflicts	Troubles among the DC factions, and conflicts about economic policy with the PLI
Segni	1953–1958	Inter-party conflicts	Conflict between the government and the PRI and PSDI over agrarian reform
Zoli	1953–1958	Intra-party conflicts	The minority cabinet keeps on to the end of the legislature, but formally resigns before it because of internal conflicts inside the DC
Fanfani II	1958–1963	Inter-party conflicts	Split in the PSDI and personal conflicts between Fanfani and the PRI leaders
Segni II	1958–1963	Inter-party conflicts	The PLI withdraws its external support mainly because of different opinions on economic policy
Tambroni	1958–1963	General vulnerability	The MSI's support for the cabinet causes social tensions and conflicts inside the DC (three ministers resign)
Fanfani III	1958–1963	Inter-party conflicts	The PSDI and PRI withdraw their external support because of the enlargement of the coalition to include the PSI decided during the DC congress

(continued)

Table 3.2 (continued)

Cabinet	Legislature	Cause of termination	Description of termination event
Fanfani IV	1958–1963	Technical reasons	After the 1963 general election, the Fanfani IV "electoral cabinet" resigns
Leone	1963–1968	Technical reasons	Bridge cabinet before a fully fledged center-left coalition can be established. In office mainly to approve the budget law
Moro	1963–1968	Inter-party conflicts	Internal conflicts over funding for private secondary education
Moro II	1963–1968	Inter-party conflicts	Internal conflicts and ensuing parliamentary defeat over a decree establishing public secondary education
Moro III	1963–1968	General vulnerability	Resignation after socialists' split, causing the withdrawal of three ministers from the cabinet
Leone II	1968–1972	Technical reasons	Transitory cabinet to renegotiate the coalition
Rumor	1968–1972	Intra-party conflicts	Problems among DC factions throughout the cabinet's duration
Rumor II	1968–1972	Inter-party conflicts	Tension between the DC and the secular parties (especially the PSI) over the divorce issue does not allow the cabinet to face parliament
Rumor III	1968–1972	General vulnerability	Impact of local election results and formation of local coalitions between the PCI and PSI
Colombo	1968–1972	Inter-party conflicts	Conflict between the PRI and DC on economic policy
Andreotti	1968–1972	Technical reasons	The cabinet does not pass the investiture vote (senate). This event causes early elections
Andreotti II	1972–1976	Inter-party conflicts	Conflict between coalition partners and strategic change decided during the DC congress
Rumor IV	1972–1976	Inter-party conflicts	Personal conflict between two ministers who are supported by their respective parties

Rumor V	1972–1976	Inter-party conflicts	One party (PSDI) asks for the end of the coalition with a number of policy criticisms. Personal conflicts are also visible
Moro IV	1972–1976	Inter-party conflicts	PSI withdraws its external support, criticizing the economic policy of the cabinet
Moro V	1972–1976	Inter-party conflicts	Troubles over economic policy; effects of the final battle on divorce, plus the effect of the Lockheed Scandal cause early elections
Andreotti III	1976–1979	Inter-party conflicts	Divisions on the question of entry into the European Monetary System
Andreotti IV	1976–1979	Technical reasons	The cabinet does not pass the investiture vote (senate)
Andreotti V	1976–1979	Technical reasons	Electoral cabinet in office for caretaking duties
Cossiga	1979–1983	Technical reasons	Prime minister resigns without parliamentary vote and is immediately reappointed, to include the PSI in the coalition after DC–PSI agreements
Cossiga II	1979–1983	Inter-party conflicts	Parliamentary cabinet defeat (lower chamber) on the economic decree
Forlani	1979–1983	General vulnerability	Abortion battle (referendum lost by Catholics) and involvement of some ministers in the P2 scandal
Spadolini	1979–1983	Intra-party conflicts	Conflicts over a decree concerning oil production, rejected by DC franchi tiratori
Spadolini II	1979–1983	Inter-party conflicts	Personal conflicts among ministers Andreatta and Formica, so-called "Comari affairs"
Fanfani V	1979–1983	Inter-party conflicts	PSI withdraws its support following a decision made during the central committee meeting
Craxi	1983–1987	General vulnerability	Cabinet defeat on its decree about local finance
Craxi II	1983–1987	Inter-party conflicts	Craxi refuses to accept the *patto della staffetta*, establishing a rotation government with Ciriaco De Mita (DC)
Fanfani VI	1983–1987	Technical reasons	The cabinet does not pass the investiture vote (lower chamber)

(continued)

Table 3.2 (continued)

Cabinet	Legislature	Cause of termination	Description of termination event
Goria	1987–1992	Inter-party conflicts	Defeat of the financial bill (already delayed out of the financial year). A number of criticisms about different policies within parties
De Mita	1987–1992	General vulnerability	Extra-parliamentary crisis determined at the end of the PSI congress
Andreotti VI	1987–1992	Intra-party conflicts	Conflict within the DC about TV regulation
Andreotti VII	1987–1992	General vulnerability	Crisis of traditional parties and outbreak of new political actors, e.g. Northern League and La Rete
Amato	1992–1994	General vulnerability	Dramatic decline in the legitimacy of the political class (*Mani Pulite* investigations)
Ciampi	1992–1994	Technical reasons	Cabinet forms only to implement electoral and economic reforms before a new early election
Berlusconi	1994–1996	Inter-party conflicts	Personal conflicts between Umberto Bossi (Northern League) and Silvio Berlusconi (Forward Italy)
Dini	1994–1996	Technical reasons	Temporary cabinet to complete some reforms before the early elections
Prodi	1996–2001	Inter-party conflicts	Policy conflicts between the Party of Communist Refoundation and Romano Prodi
D'Alema	1996–2001	Inter-party conflicts	SDI withdraws from the cabinet, arguing that D'Alema is too uncharismatic to win the next general election
D'Alema II	1996–2001	Inter-party conflicts	D'Alema resigns after heavy losses in the regional elections. Analysts attribute the defeat of the ruling coalition to internal strife
Amato II	1996–2001	Technical reasons	Electoral cabinet in office for caretaking duties
Berlusconi II	2001–2006	Inter-party conflicts	UDC withdraws from the coalition over Berlusconi's refusal to amend the government program or call early elections

Berlusconi III	2001–2006	General vulnerability	Berlusconi isdefeated in the 2006 Italian general election
Prodi II	2006–2008	Inter-party conflicts	Prodi's is defeated in a confidence vote (senate). Key role played by UDEUR and Liberal Democrats
Berlusconi IV	2008–2013	General vulnerability	Berlusconi resigns amidst pressure from the Northern League, the finance minister, and from the president of the Republic due to economy
Monti	2008–2013	Inter-party conflicts	Monti resigns after passing the 2013 budget, having lost the external support of the PDL the month prior
Letta	2013–2018	Intra-party conflicts	Letta resigns after losing a vote of no confidence undertaken by the PD party executive
Renzi	2013–2018	General vulnerability	Renzi resigns after defeat in the constitutional referendum of December 4, 2016
Gentiloni	2013–2018	Technical reasons	Gentiloni resigns in the run-up to the 2018 general election
Conte	2018–2022	Inter-party conflicts	The results of the 2019 European election prompt the League's leader Salvini to claim greater room for maneuver
Conte II	2018–2022	Inter-party conflicts	Tension between Prime Minister Conte and Matteo Renzi over the pandemic management and intelligence services
Draghi	2018–2022	Inter-party conflicts	Tension between Prime Minister Draghi and supporting parties over the so-called "Decreto Aiuti"

Source: Updated from Improta (2022b).

One of the most striking features is the prominence of inter-party conflicts as the leading cause of terminations. This is evident in many instances, starting as early as De Gasper IV in 1951, when the Partito Socialista Democratico Italiano (PSDI) decided to leave the coalition, and continuing through the more recent examples like Prodi II and Draghi. In these cases, it is clear that coalition governments, while necessary to govern in Italy's proportional electoral system, are also inherently fragile, regardless of the political ideological positioning of the cabinet. The need to balance competing interests among various political actors often leads to irreconcilable differences. For instance, Draghi's government fell apart when tensions between coalition partners became too pronounced, particularly regarding disagreements over the economic relief measures introduced in the "Decreto Aiuti." This reflects a broader trend in which governments are vulnerable to collapse when inter-party alliances begin to unravel.

In addition to conflicts between different parties, intra-party conflicts – disputes within the same ruling party – also feature heavily as a cause of government instability. Intra-party turmoil was a critical factor in the resignation of governments like that of Letta in 2014, who was ousted after a no-confidence vote by his own party (Partito Democratico; PD). This example shows that even within the leading political force of a coalition, internal divisions can destabilize an entire government. When party leaders cannot maintain cohesion within their ranks, their government's ability to stay in power is significantly compromised.

Beyond conflicts, both between and within parties, many cabinets have succumbed to general vulnerability, a concept that captures the weakening of political legitimacy or broader social and economic challenges. For instance, Berlusconi IV (2011) resigned due to mounting economic pressures during the Eurozone crisis and the loss of support from crucial coalition members like the Lega Nord. In these cases, the general vulnerability made it difficult for governments to continue, irrespective of specific party dynamics.

There is also a notable frequency of cabinets ending for technical reasons, which often relate to procedural issues or caretaker governments awaiting new elections. These terminations are less politically relevant and tend to occur when a government fails to secure an investiture vote or is temporarily in office to manage the transition between elections. For instance, Gentiloni (2018) stepped down ahead of the 2018 elections in a "routine" move.

While inter-party conflicts are the most common cause, often magnified by electoral results or shifts in public opinion, Table 3.2 also reveals that cabinet conflicts and general vulnerability often act as compounding factors. The overlapping pressures can result in governments being unable to respond effectively, leading to their eventual termination.

In conclusion, Italy's trajectories regarding cabinet termination are characterized by frequent struggles to maintain stability due to the ingrained complexity of coalition governance. Inter-party conflicts stand out as the most recurrent issue, but intra-party conflicts and general vulnerability also play important roles in destabilizing governments.

Chapter 4
Who did what? Government instability
and policymaking accountability

This chapter deals with the nexus between government instability and policymaking accountability in Italy. It does so by examining the policy proposals' initiators and terminators to highlight how the policy cycle is affected by cabinet turnover, reducing citizens' ability to identify government responsibility, thus reducing government accountability.

1 The problem of responsibility attribution

The attribution of responsibility is fundamental to democratic governance, as it allows citizens to hold their leaders accountable based on the policies they implement and the outcomes of such policies. In a stable political system, this process is relatively straightforward: voters can identify which parties or leaders are responsible for specific actions, assess the impact of these actions, and make (ideally) informed choices at the ballot box according to a "punishment or reward" mechanism. However, in countries like Italy, where government instability is a persistent issue, responsibility attribution becomes much more complex, making it difficult for responsibility attribution to be clear in the country and ultimately undermining government accountability.

This is a crucial problem, as in a democracy responsibility attribution is a fundamental mechanism through which voters can evaluate government performance. The basic premise is that citizens can observe government actions, understand the consequences of these actions, and assign credit or blame to the political actors responsible for them. This process is relevant because it incentivizes politicians to act in ways that align with the public interest; those who perform well should be rewarded with reelection, while those who fail are voted out of office.

However, this ideal scenario assumes a stable political environment where the roles of different political actors are clear, the policy process is transparent, and information is available to the public without restrictions. In such a context, voters can trace the link between decisions and outcomes, making responsibility attribution relatively easy. In contrast, in a setting characterized by frequent government turnover and complex coalition politics – such as Italy – these conditions are often

https://doi.org/10.1515/9783111329727-005

not met, making it difficult for citizens to accurately determine who is responsible for policy outcomes.

Frequent changes in the composition and leadership of the government, often due to coalition breakdowns, government crises, and early elections, are a common feature of the Italian political system. Italian government instability has profound implications for the process of responsibility attribution. Assessing a stable government, citizens can easily link specific policies to the actors who implemented them, enabling clear government and policymaking accountability. In a context of instability, where governments change frequently, this link is broken. When a new government takes office, it often shifts policy priorities, and ongoing initiatives may be abandoned or altered. Consequently, voters may struggle to determine who should be credited or blamed for particular outcomes, especially when multiple governments have had a role in shaping them.

For instance, the rapid succession of governments in Italy has often led to the fragmentation of policy initiatives. One government might begin a policy, but before its effects can be fully realized a new government may take over, possibly altering or even reversing the policy direction. This discontinuity not only disrupts the policy implementation process but also creates confusion among citizens over which political actors are responsible for the outcomes.

The policy cycle typically involves several stages: agenda-setting, policy formulation, decision-making, implementation, and evaluation. In a stable government, these stages are usually managed by a consistent set of actors, allowing for a coherent and traceable process. However, in Italy the frequent changes in government mean that different stages of the policy cycle are often handled by different cabinets, leading to a fragmented and inconsistent policy process.

For example, a government may initiate a significant reform, but before it can be fully implemented the government falls and a new administration takes over. The new government may not share the same priorities or may seek to distance itself from its predecessor, leading to alterations of the policy. As a result, the policy cycle is disrupted, and it becomes difficult for citizens to attribute responsibility.

The lack of effective responsibility attribution when it comes to the policy cycle is particularly evident in Italy's economic and social policies, where long-term planning and sustained implementation are crucial. For instance, pension reforms, labor market regulations, and public-spending policies often require a consistent approach over several years to be effective. However, in Italy these policies have frequently been subject to abrupt changes due to government instability, making it difficult to evaluate their success or failure and to hold any particular government accountable.

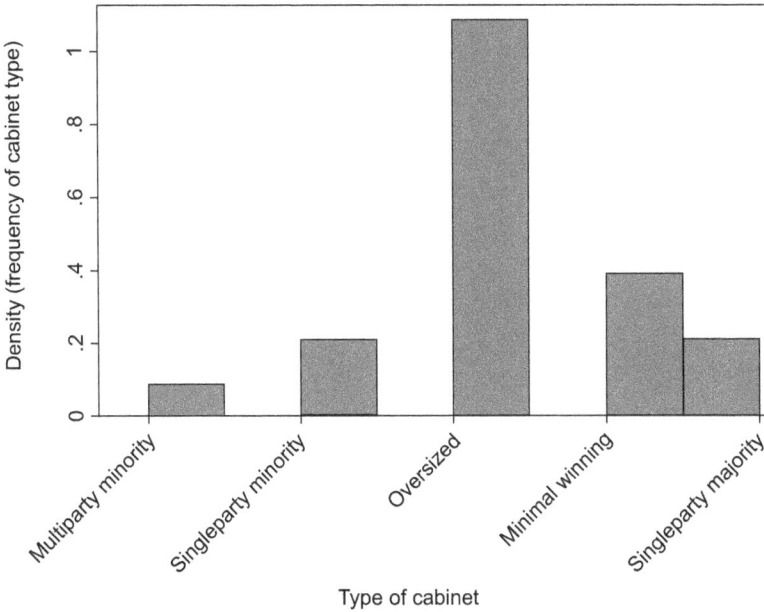

Figure 4.1: Type of cabinet in Italy.
Source: Own elaboration.

Coalition governments are a common feature of Italian government formation, largely due to the proportional representation electoral system, which makes it difficult for any single party to gain an outright majority. As shown in Figure 4.1, the establishment of an oversized majority coalition has been the most recurrent outcome of government formations in Italy. Coalition governments complicate the process of responsibility attribution, and Italian governments have often found themselves in such ruling configurations. The establishment of multiparty and single-party minority cabinets has been more limited, as have single-party majority governments.[5] In a coalition, multiple parties share power, and the responsibilities for different policy areas are divided among relevant ministries. This division of labor can blur the lines of accountability, as it may not be clear which party is responsible for specific decisions, especially when cases of "ministerial drift" (Indridason & Kam, 2008) occur. Moreover, in Italy coalition partners often have different ideological positions and policy preferences, leading to compromises that may dilute the clarity of policy initiatives.

---

5 In this regard, single-party majority governments were formed only through the external support of vital external parties, which however did not occupy ministerial offices.

This situation is further complicated by the frequent collapse of coalitions in Italy. When a coalition terminates prematurely, the parties involved may engage in blame-shifting, each accusing the other of causing the government's collapse or policy failures, as in the case of the first Conte cabinet when the M5S and the Lega clashed over policy-related issues. This blame-shifting aggravates accountability.

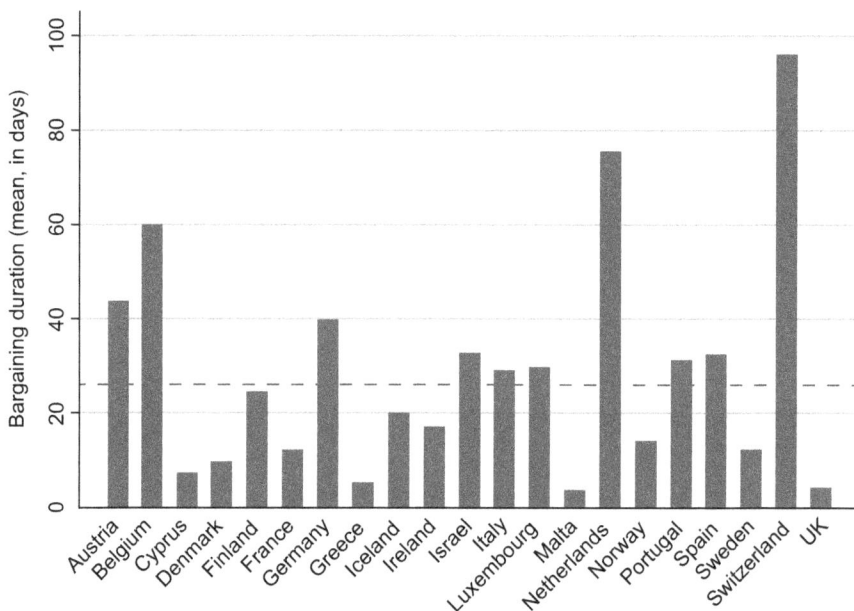

Figure 4.2: Bargaining duration per country.
Source: Own elaboration.

Moreover, the complexity of coalition negotiations often means that policies are the result of compromises that do not fully satisfy any of the coalition partners. Figure 4.2 shows the average bargaining duration during the government formation stage. As observed, Italy is among the countries spending more time on negotiations in comparative perspective. When policies promoted by a conflictual coalition fail or are unpopular, it is difficult for voters to identify which party should be blamed if the lines of accountability are blurred.

One prominent example of policy discontinuity in Italy is the country's approach to pension reform (Franco, 2002). Over the years, Italian governments have introduced various pension reforms aimed at addressing the sustainability of the public pension system. However, each new government has tended to revise or overturn the reforms introduced by its predecessor, leading to a cycle of policy reversals (Franco & Tommasino, 2020). This discontinuity has not only created uncertainty for workers but has also made it difficult for voters to determine which government is responsible for the long-term viability of the pension system.

Finally, the problem of responsibility attribution also involves the media system. The frequent changes in government incentivize the media to adjust their coverage to reflect the changing political situation. This can result in a focus on short-term issues, such as scandals, leadership changes, and intra-coalition conflicts, rather than on substantive policy debates and programs. This focus on the short term can obscure the broader policy context.

2 Governmental agendas and policy initiatives

This section empirically explores "who did what" in terms of policy implementation, considering the problem of responsibility attribution and the frequent government turnover in Italy. In it, I aim to trace policy discontinuity, where reforms are proposed by one government but only implemented by subsequent administrations. This pattern complicates the process of governance and raises significant issues concerning responsibility attribution – who should be credited or blamed for the success or failure of these reforms.

Table 4.1 shows how policy initiatives have often been carried across multiple governments. Many prime ministers, particularly in the post-war period, held office for only brief periods before being replaced. This instability meant that governments often had insufficient time to fully implement their policy agendas. For example, the short tenures of Pella and Fanfani left little opportunity for such leaders to see their reforms through to completion.

This high turnover creates a scenario where reforms are proposed but not immediately enacted, leaving them to be addressed by subsequent governments. As a result, the continuity of policy initiatives is often disrupted, with new governments potentially altering, delaying, or even abandoning the reforms set in motion by their predecessors. This disruption can undermine the effectiveness of reforms and create confusion among the public regarding which government is responsible for particular policy outcomes.

A clear pattern in Table 4.1 is the frequent implementation of reforms by administrations different from those that initially proposed them. For instance, Zoli's pension reform proposal in 1957–1958 was only partially realized under the later government of Fanfani II. Similarly, Rumor's workers' Statute, introduced during

Table 4.1: Policy discontinuity in Italy.

Prime minister	Time in office	Key reform proposed	Reform implemented by the same government?	Reform implemented by a subsequent government?
Alcide De Gasperi	1948–1953	Land Reform Act (1950)	Yes	–
Giuseppe Pella	1953–1954	Monetary stability measures	Yes	–
Amintore Fanfani I	1954	Public housing initiative	**No**	**Yes, implemented in later Fanfani governments**
Mario Scelba	1954–1955	Public Order Law	Yes	–
Antonio Segni I	1955–1957	Agrarian reform continuation	Yes	–
Adone Zoli	1957–1958	Pension reform proposal	**No**	**Yes, partially under Fanfani II**
Amintore Fanfani II	1958–1959	Education reform proposal	**No**	**Yes, under Moro I (1963–1968)**
Antonio Segni II	1959–1960	Continued agrarian reforms	Yes	–
Fernando Tambroni	1960	Economic development Southern Italy (Cassa per il Mezzogiorno)	Yes	–
Amintore Fanfani III	1960–1963	Public works and housing	Yes	–

Giovanni Leone I	1963	Budgetary discipline	Yes	–
Aldo Moro I	1963–1968	Education reform (1962), Implementation of nationalization of energy	Yes	–
Giovanni Leone II	1968	Economic stabilization	Yes	–
Mariano Rumor I	1968–1969	Workers; Statute (Statuto dei Lavoratori) introduction	**No**	**Yes, implemented under Rumor II**
Mariano Rumor II	1969–1970	Workers' Statute	Yes	–
Mariano Rumor III	1970–1972	Economic development measures	Yes	–
Giulio Andreotti I	1972–1973	Anti-inflation measures	Yes	–
Giulio Andreotti II	1973	Continued economic policies	Yes	–
Mariano Rumor IV	1973–1974	Public works expansion	Yes	–
Mariano Rumor V	1974	Divorce Law implementation	Yes	–
Aldo Moro II	1974–1976	Divorce Law implementation, Economic stability measures	Yes	–

(continued)

Table 4.1 (continued)

Prime minister	Time in office	Key reform proposed	Reform implemented by the same government?	Reform implemented by a subsequent government?
Aldo Moro III	1976	Continued economic stabilization	Yes	–
Giulio Andreotti III	1976–1978	Anti-terrorism measures	Yes	–
Giulio Andreotti IV	1978–1979	Continued anti-terrorism measures	Yes	–
Giulio Andreotti V	1979	Economic stabilization	Yes	–
Francesco Cossiga I	1979–1980	Anti-terrorism laws	Yes	–
Francesco Cossiga II	1980	Continued anti-terrorism laws	Yes	–
Arnaldo Forlani	1980–1981	Public administration reform	Yes	–
Giovanni Spadolini I	1981–1982	Anti-corruption measures	**No**	**Yes, continued under Craxi I**
Giovanni Spadolini II	1982	Continued anti-corruption measures	Yes	–

Amintore Fanfani IV	1982–1983	Economic stabilization	Yes	–
Bettino Craxi I	1983–1986	Wage indexation reform	Yes	–
Bettino Craxi II	1986–1987	Labor market reform	Yes	–
Amintore Fanfani V	1987	Fiscal stabilization measures	Yes	–
Giovanni Goria	1987–1988	Fiscal reform proposals	No	**Yes, under later Andreotti government**
Ciriaco De Mita	1988–1989	Justice system reform	No	**Yes, under Andreotti VI**
Giulio Andreotti VI	1989–1991	European integration initiatives	Yes	–
Giulio Andreotti VII	1991–1992	Budgetary discipline, Maastricht Treaty preparations	Yes	–
Giuliano Amato I	1992–1993	Pension reform, Anti-corruption legislation	Yes	–
Carlo Azeglio Ciampi	1993–1994	Economic stabilization, Euro adoption preparation	Yes	–
Silvio Berlusconi I	1994–1995	Justice system reform, Media deregulation	No	**Yes, justice reform revisited in later terms**

(continued)

Table 4.1 (continued)

Prime minister	Time in office	Key reform proposed	Reform implemented by the same government?	Reform implemented by a subsequent government?
Lamberto Dini	1995–1996	Pension reform	Yes	–
Romano Prodi I	1996–1998	Euro adoption, Public administration reform	**No (Euro adoption)**	**Yes, Euro adoption finalized under D'Alema I**
Massimo D'Alema I	1998–1999	Kosovo War, Electoral law reform	**No (Electoral law reform)**	**Yes (Electoral law reform further addressed in later governments)**
Massimo D'Alema II	1999–2000	Continued Kosovo War involvement, Economic measures	Yes	–
Giuliano Amato II	2000–2001	Anti-terrorism measures post-9/11	Yes	–
Silvio Berlusconi II	2001–2005	Constitutional reform (2005)	**No, defeated in referendum (2006)**	–
Silvio Berlusconi III	2005–2006	Economic recovery plan	Yes	–
Romano Prodi II	2006–2008	Economic reforms, Reduction of public debt	Yes	–
Silvio Berlusconi IV	2008–2011	Anti-immigration measures, Justice reform	Yes	–

Mario Monti	2011–2013	Austerity measures, Labor market reform	Yes	–	–
Enrico Letta	2013–2014	Institutional reform proposals	No	No	No
Matteo Renzi	2014–2016	Constitutional reform (2016), Jobs Act	**No, constitutional reform defeated in referendum (2016)**	**No**	**Jobs Act implemented successfully**
Paolo Gentiloni	2016–2018	Economic stability measures, Migrant crisis management	Yes	–	–
Giuseppe Conte I	2018–2019	Citizenship income (Reddito di Cittadinanza)	Yes	–	–
Giuseppe Conte II	2019–2021	Covid-19 response, Green transition policies	Yes	–	–
Mario Draghi	2021–2022	Covid-19 recovery plan, Fiscal stability measures	Yes	–	–
Giorgia Meloni	2022-present	Immigration policy reform, Fiscal policy overhaul	Ongoing	–	–

his first term (1968–1969), was fully implemented during his second term (1969–1970). This indicates a reliance on subsequent governments to carry forward the legislative and policy agendas of their predecessors. This complicates the attribution of responsibility. When a policy is implemented by a different government from the one that proposed it, it becomes unclear which administration should be held accountable for its success or failure. This ambiguity can dilute government accountability, as the original proponents of the reform might argue that the policy was altered or implemented under different circumstances, thus absolving themselves of any negative outcomes. Conversely, the implementing government might claim credit for the successful execution of a reform, even if they merely finalized a process that had begun under a previous administration.

From Table 4.1, we can observe several examples of responsibility attribution problems. Renzi's administration proposed various reforms, including a constitutional reform. The constitutional reform aimed to significantly streamline Italy's political system, including reducing the powers of the senate and altering the division of responsibilities between the state and the regions. However, this reform was met with significant opposition and was ultimately defeated in a 2016 referendum. After this proposal, Italy embarked on other constitutional reform attempts, which contributed to increasing the long tradition of constitutional redesign (yet with several failures) in the country. Similarly, in his later terms Berlusconi governments focused on anti-immigration measures and justice reform. While his government did implement some aspects of these reforms, the full extent of the justice reform – intended, *inter alia*, to reduce the length of trials – remained incomplete. Successive governments revisited the justice system, but Berlusconi's initial efforts were overshadowed.

A prime example of problems of responsibility attribution is the Conte governmental experience. Conte served as prime minister in two governments: first in a coalition between the M5S and the Lega (2018–2019) and then in a coalition between the M5S and the PD (2019–2021). Conte's first government focused on the introduction of Citizenship Income (Reddito di Cittadinanza), aimed at providing financial support to the unemployed and economically disadvantaged. While Citizenship Income was envisaged during Conte's first term in office, its effectiveness and sustainability were questioned and adjustments were needed during subsequent terms. As a result, these policies were handed over to Draghi's and then Meloni's cabinets. This diffusion of responsibility has made it complex to assess the effectiveness of Citizenship Income in Italy.

3 The instability–accountability nexus: The wavering path of the governmental policy cycle

As discussed above, Italian government instability often derives from the challenge of governing conflictual coalitions. Coalition governments are more fragile, especially in a polarized and fragmented system like Italy's. Government crises have been frequent and they have significant implication for policy continuity and the governmental policy cycle. As we have observed, reforms proposed by one government are often left unfinished or abandoned when a new administration takes over, leading to a lack of long-term strategic political planning. In this section, I analyze the key crises that have affected recent governments.

In Italy, coalition governments are the norm. The necessity of coalition-building has introduced a significant degree of fragility into the already fragile Italian political system. Coalition partners have frequently found themselves in critical conflicting situations, triggering government crises that result in early elections and formations of new governments. For example, in 2018 the Conte I government was sworn in. Key policies were Citizenship Income and "Quota 100" pension reform, which allowed workers to retire earlier, at the age of 62, provided they had at least 38 years of contributions. These reforms were emblematic of the coalition program signed by the M5S and the League, titled "Contratto per il governo del cambiamento" (Contract for the government of change). However, despite the initial success in passing the proposal stages of the reforms, the coalition between the two challenger parties was inherently unstable due to critical ideological heterogeneity. These differences soon led to significant internal conflicts.

The first major crisis occurred in August 2019, when Matteo Salvini, leader of the League, sensing an opportunity to capitalize on his party's growing popularity in the opinion polls, withdrew his support from the government in an attempt to elicit early elections. Salvini's gambit backfired, as the M5S quickly moved to form a new coalition with the center-left PD, thus sidelining Salvini and preventing early elections. This marked the end of the Conte I government and the beginning of the Conte II government. The crisis that brought down the first Conte government not only interrupted the policy agenda of that administration but also highlighted the fragility of coalitions in Italy, particularly when based on a narrow convergence of interests rather than a shared ideological vision, as often occurs in Italy.

The Conte II government inherited several ongoing policy initiatives from the previous cabinet, which was spearheaded by Conte himself but with different ideological stances. In particular, the Conte II government had to continue the implementation of Citizenship Income and Quota 100 reforms. However, the most significant challenge that this government faced was the Covid-19 pandemic, which began in early 2020. To counter this health emergency, the government had to develop the Recovery and Resilience Plan (PNRR), which was part of the European Union's broader Covid-19 recovery strategy. The PNRR outlined how Italy would use the funds allocated to it under the EU's Recovery Fund. Despite this delicate situation, the Conte II government faced internal conflicts as well. Tensions between the M5S and the partners emerged over several policy issues. In January 2021, Matteo Renzi withdrew his party's support from the government, primarily due to disagreements over the management of EU funds. Renzi's move triggered a government crisis that ultimately led to Conte's resignation. Despite efforts to form a new coalition, it became clear that Conte could not secure again a majority in the senate, leading to his decision to step down. This crisis once again disrupted the policymaking process, particularly regarding the implementation of the PNRR.

In the wake of Conte's resignation, Italian president Sergio Mattarella turned to Mario Draghi, former president of the European Central Bank, to form a new government. Draghi's government was a national unity one that included almost all major political parties, except for Brothers of Italy (Giorgia Meloni's party) and Italian Left (Nicola Fratoianni's party). Internal conflicts persisted even in this unitary ruling configuration. As the pandemic crisis began to recede and attention shifted towards the recovery phase, coalition partners started positioning themselves for the next general election. This led to tensions within the cabinet, particularly over issues such as economic policy, support and intervention in the Russia–Ukraine war, and the distribution of EU funds. The umpteenth government crisis led to the termination of the Draghi government in July 2022. Draghi's resignation disrupted several key reforms, particularly those tied to the PNRR. The political instability provoked the scaling back of reforms. The responsibility for their implementation was passed on to the next government.

The last instance of diluted government accountability is constituted by the formation of the Meloni government. This government represents a marked shift to the right, and it inherited a series of challenges from Draghi and Conte, including the implementation of the PNRR and the Russia–Ukraine war. Policy continuity is particularly crucial for the effective implementation of the PNRR, which was developed by Conte, initially managed by Draghi, and now started to be implemented by Meloni. When the voters eventually evaluate the overall cycle of the PNRR, who will be blamed or rewarded for it?

Overall, the history of Italian governments highlights the persistent challenge of government instability. Recently, the pattern of government crises has recurrently interrupted the policymaking process. This instability has aggravated existing difficulties in achieving continuity in governance, complicating the problem of responsibility attribution. Constitutional engineering efforts should promote measures to strengthen mechanisms that ensure coalition cohesion, establishing clear procedures for solving internal disputes. Finally, there is a need for a more long-term-oriented approach over short-term political gains (Improta & Mannoni, 2024). As the country must deal with problems of debt sustainability, abandoning short-termism should constitute the main concern of all parties that seek to occupy governmental posts.

Chapter 5
Explanatory drivers: Between party conflicts and general vulnerability

This chapter empirically examines the drivers of government instability by employing Cox survival analysis. It identifies factors leading to increased risk of termination, particularly in terms of party conflicts and general vulnerability of the Italian political system.

1 Causes of government termination

As we observed in Chapter 3, Italian governments have long been characterized by a remarkable level of instability, often marked by frequent changes in the driving seat of governments. The key causes behind the termination of Italian governments focus on two major explanatory drivers: party conflicts and general vulnerability. The former can manifest both as inter-party and intra-party conflicts. Inter-party conflicts arise between different coalition parties and typically stem from disagreements over major policy issues, such as economic reform and foreign policy postures. Intra-party conflicts, on the other hand, arise within a party of the coalition, where factionalism and sometimes even personal rivalries undermine the party's ability to maintain coalition unity and support for the government. Beyond party conflicts, the general vulnerability of the Italian political system has been crucial in driving governments' early terminations. This vulnerability is shaped by political and social factors that weaken the legitimacy of governments to rule effectively, even when vulnerability is exacerbated by external pressures.

By considering the trajectories of the causes of government termination in Italy displayed in Chapter 3, I advance some hypotheses to empirically examine factors which might influence the instability of Italian governments. Hence, based on the above-mentioned premises, two key hypotheses can be formulated to explain government termination in Italy.

H1: Governments with higher levels of inter-party conflicts face an increased risk of termination. Therefore, as conflicts between coalition parties over issues (regarding, for instance, policy) intensify, the likelihood of government early collapse increases, particularly during more unstable periods (i.e., First and Third Republics).

https://doi.org/10.1515/9783111329727-006

H2: Governments ruling in periods of heightened vulnerability are more likely to collapse. Political and social turmoil weaken the capacity of governments to maintain support, increasing the risk of termination.

All in all, the termination of Italian governments should be primarily driven by two factors: conflicts and vulnerability. These dynamics would signal the rooted fragmented nature of the Italian political system.

2 Italian governments' survival analysis

A survival analysis of Italian governments has been performed to test the hypotheses presented above. As a proxy to gauge the impact of party conflicts, I used the Effective Number of Government Parties index, originally collected based on the Effective Number of Parties introduced by Laakso and Taagepera (1979). As proxies for political and social turmoil, I used the index of trust in parties and the political corruption index. I have used the political corruption index from the Varieties of Democracy (V-Dem) Dataset (Coppedge et al., 2021) – the variable captures citizens' perception of how corrupt a political system is. The trust in parties is a variable from the European Social Survey. It measures how much citizens trust political parties in a specific political system.

Before exploring the appropriateness of the hypothesized mechanisms, it is worth looking at the different survival rates of the three periods of Italian Republican history. As the survival curves in Figure 5.1 illustrate, governments in the Second Republic had generally longer tenures compared with those in the First and Third Republics. The median survival time for government in the First Republic was notably lower than that of the Second Republic, indicating that reforms to the electoral system had some success in prolonging government lifespans. However, fragmentation and intra-coalition conflicts remained challenges in both periods, suggesting that the reforms were only partially effective in addressing the root causes of instability, as discussed in earlier sections of the book.

Moving to hypothesis-testing (Figure 5.2), I hypothesized that the effective number of government parties serves as a key predictor of Italian government instability, with a higher number of parties increasing transaction costs and room for conflicts, in turn increasing the likelihood of government early termination. The survival curves show that as the effective number of government parties increases, the probability of government survival decreases significantly. Governments with fewer coalition partners tend to survive longer, while those with more parties experience higher risks of early collapse. This finding confirms my first hypothesis

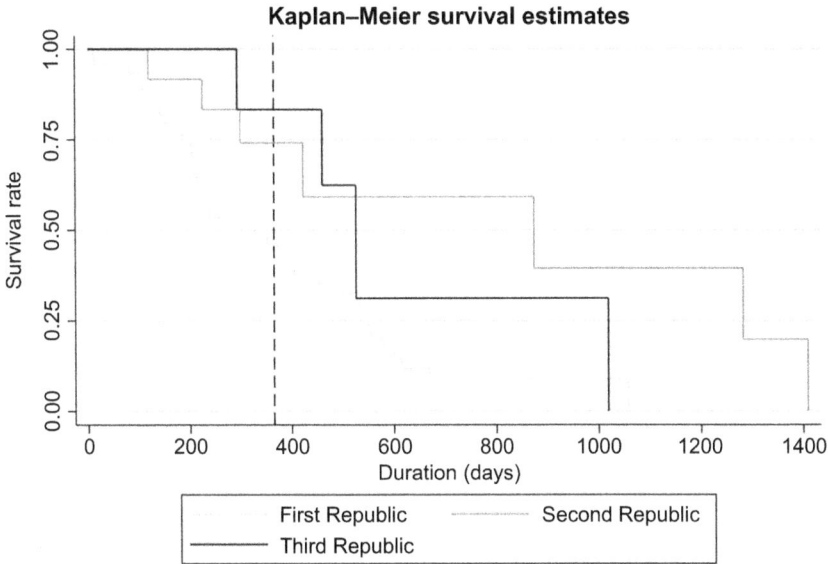

Figure 5.1: Survival estimates per 'Republic'.
Note: Reference line: 365 days in office.
Source: Own elaboration.

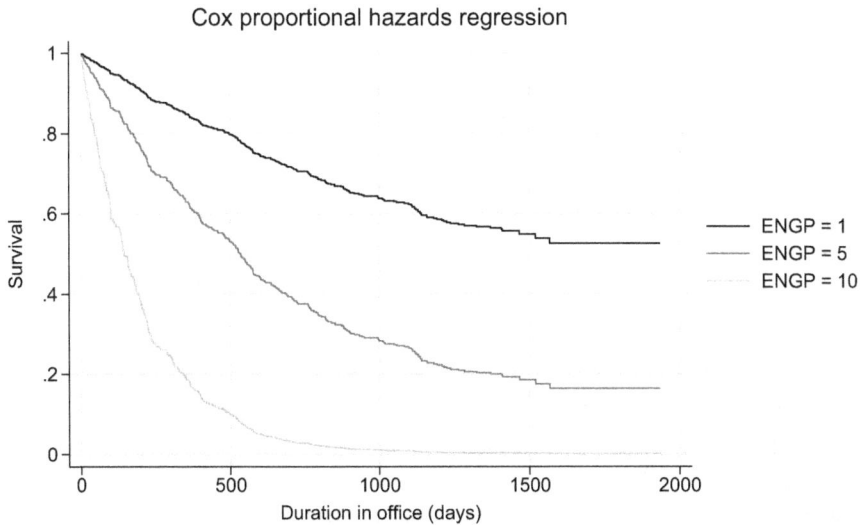

Figure 5.2: Cox regression of fragmentation in government.
Source: Own elaboration.

and the theoretical assumption that managing a larger number of parties within a coalition leads to greater internal disagreements and ultimately government instability.

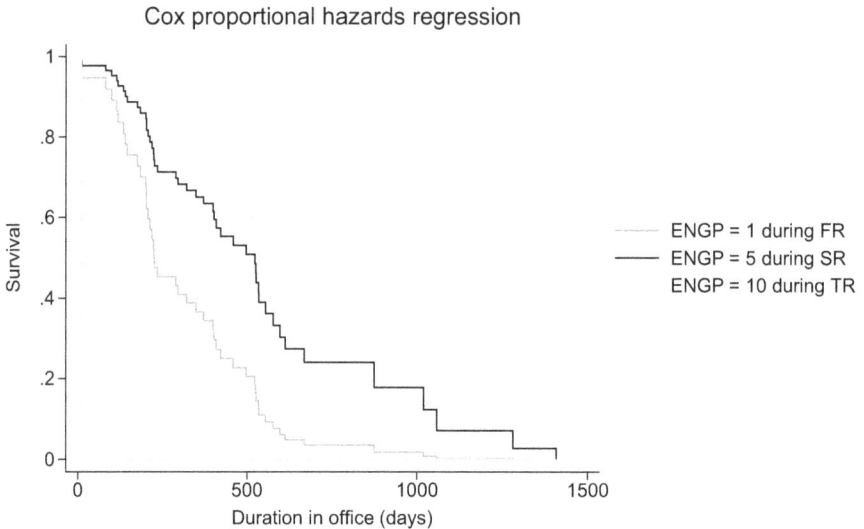

Figure 5.3: Cox regression of fragmentation in government interacted with Republic.
Source: Own elaboration.

When considering the interaction between the effective number of government parties and the type of Republic (First, Second, Third), we observe a significant difference in how this variable affects government survival in the three periods (Figure 5.3). In the First Republic, in particular, the presence of a large number of coalition parties was a more immediate threat to government survival, with survival rates dropping sharply as the number of partners increased. This can be attributed to the lack of institutional mechanisms to manage coalition conflicts and the weak party discipline that characterized the period.

In contrast, in the Second Republic, while fragmentation still reduced government survival, the effects were less pronounced. The institutional reforms of the 1990s, such as the introduction of majoritarian components, helped mitigate some of the instability associated with the previous period. The survival curves indicate that governments in the Second Republic could endure for slightly longer, despite higher fragmentation.

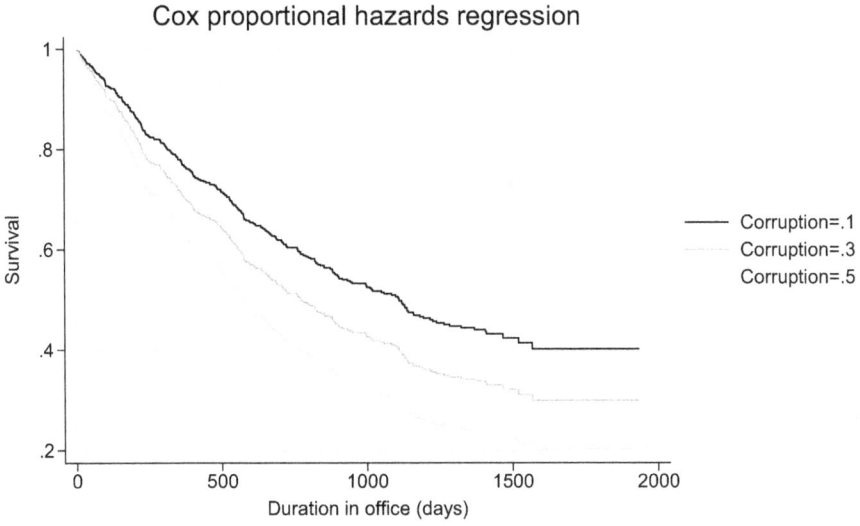

Figure 5.4: Cox regression of corruption.
Source: Own elaboration.

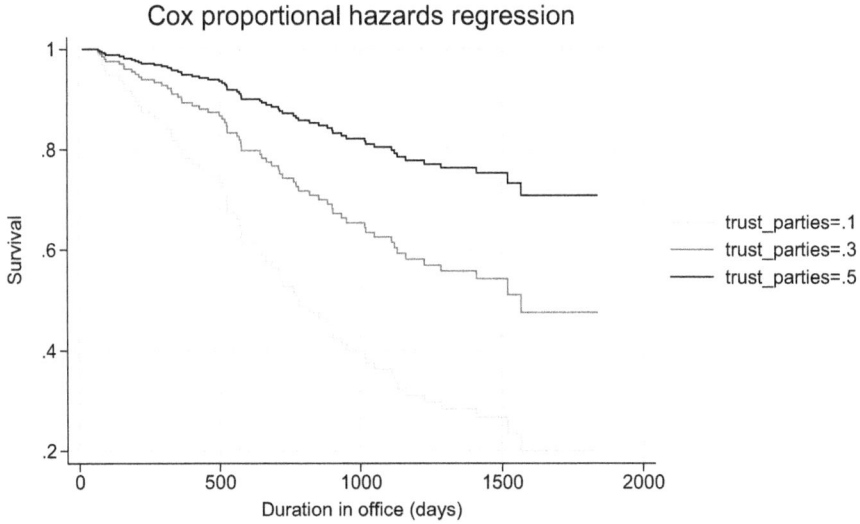

Figure 5.5: Cox regression of trust.
Source: Own elaboration.

Moving to H2, I hypothesized that trust in parties and corruption could be significant drivers of government instability, with higher levels of trust and lower levels of corruption associated with longer government tenures. The survival curves demonstrate a clear pattern: governments ruling in environments characterized by high trust and low corruption are more likely to survive. In contrast, governments operating in contexts of low trust and high corruption face higher risks of early termination. The logic behind this finding is that when citizens have little trust in political parties, governments may struggle to maintain legitimacy and are more vulnerable to internal and external pressures. Similarly, high levels of corruption can erode the credibility of ruling parties and potentially trigger crises that lead to their collapse.

All in all, the survival analysis of Italian governments highlighted critical factors influencing government instability in the country. Historically, the First Republic was marked by extreme government instability. The situation improved in the Second Republic, yet the Third Republic has witnessed a return of shorter government lifespans, exemplified by the rapid turnover of governments led by Giuseppe Conte and Mario Draghi. The survival analysis confirmed that party conflicts and general vulnerability (exemplified by scandals like Tangentopoli) erode government tenure, increasing the risk of government early collapse. These findings suggest that while reforms have helped, deeper institutional changes, such as strengthening party discipline, are necessary for long-term stability in Italy.

In the next chapter, I aim to offer some evidence-based guidance for solving the instability problem.

Chapter 6
How to solve instability? Institutional remedies and policy recommendations

Adopting a constitutional engineering perspective, this chapter illustrates the possible institutional remedies – also borrowing from successful comparative cases – for the instability issue. It provides policy recommendations to policymakers and all those involved in the political process in the country.

1 Uncertainty and conflict reduction

For a long time, the proportional representation system enacted in Italy has fostered the emergence and consolidation of different political cultures, eliciting pluralism. However, it has also led to fragmented coalitions and difficulties in maintaining stability in office. Therefore, considering the global challenges of contemporary democracies (Improta & Mannoni, 2024), Italy must reduce uncertainty and conflicts, addressing the issue of fragmentation and instability through the introduction of necessary reforms.

One of the primary causes of government instability in Italy is the ingrained uncertainty and conflict within coalition governments. The process of building and maintaining coalitions, especially in a highly fragmented party system like the Italian one, involves constant negotiation and compromise between diverse (and often conflicting) political goals and incentives. This often results in internal coalition disputes, where smaller parties exert disproportionate influence, threatening to withdraw their support unless their specific demands are met. Such dynamics can lead to a level of conflict that culminates in early government collapses, as coalitions are unable to maintain cohesion over time.

From a comparative perspective, countries like Germany and Spain have successfully reduced uncertainty and coalition conflict by adopting institutional tools and rules that enhance stability. Germany's mixed electoral system, which combines proportional representation with single-member districts, ensures that coalitions may be less fragmented. Moreover, the constructive vote of no confidence (discussed in Section 2) further reduces the risk of abrupt government termination by ensuring that no government is ousted without a ready replacement.

In the Italian context, uncertainty can be reduced through several reforms that aim to reduce fragmentation and reinforce the stability of coalition governments.

https://doi.org/10.1515/9783111329727-007

First, a central issue contributing to instability is the adoption of the proportional representation system, which allows small parties to enter parliament and (often) hold the balance of power in coalition negotiations. To reduce fragmentation, Italy could adopt an electoral system that encourages the formation of more cohesive coalitions, while still maintaining a degree of proportionality to reflect the preferences of voters.

In this regard, there would be a need for the introduction of higher electoral thresholds. For example, Italy could raise the minimum vote share required for a party to gain representation in parliament from its current level (3%) to 5%, like the thresholds in place in Germany and several other European countries. This would prevent small, fringe parties from entering parliament, reducing the number of coalition partners (which is critical when it comes to bargaining) and making it easier to form stable governments. A higher threshold would discourage the proliferation of minor parties which are often equipped with blackmail potential (Sartori, 1976).

Another option would be to adopt a mixed-member electoral system, where half of the seats in parliament are filled through single-member districts (which favor larger parties) and the other half through proportional representation (which allows for a higher degree of pluralism). This system balances the need for enhanced representativeness of the system with the need for stable governments, ensuring that ruling parties are incentivized to cooperate and can benefit from reduced uncertainty. The adoption of smaller constituencies for the single-member district component could also mitigate regional political fragmentation, incentivizing parties to reduce their efforts in seeking territorial support.

Political science has also highlighted the role of coalition agreements (Klüver et al., 2023). Along these lines, a useful reform would be the formalization and strengthening of coalition agreements. Although coalition agreements have been attempted in Italy, such as during the Conte I government, they have not always succeeded in mitigating conflicts between coalition partners. However, formalizing the adoption of coalition agreements (at both the pre-election and post-election levels) could still play an important role in fostering long-term, systemic stability. Such agreements would provide a clear programmatic framework that binds coalition partners to a shared agenda, reducing room for divergence and internal disputes. That might not work well for each individual cabinet, yet if we adopt a systemic perspective we could still observe some increase in stability. Also, by encouraging political parties to formalize coalitions before elections, voters would have a clearer understanding of potential governing arrangements, and parties would be bound by a pre-established policy platform. This would reduce post-election bargaining and uncertainty, as coalition partners would have already agreed on key issues before taking office. In countries like Austria, pre-electoral coalition agreements have helped streamline the process of government formation and reduced intra-coalition conflict. Additionally, post-electoral coalition agreements should also be helpful if mechanisms that ensure adherence to the agreed-upon agenda are envisaged. For instance, coalition agreements could include binding arbitration mechanisms for resolving disputes.

To mitigate internal coalition disputes, it is also necessary to strengthen the mandate of the prime minister. In Italy, coalition partners often wield veto power over government decisions, leading to frequent deadlocks and crises. To prevent this, the prime minister's authority to manage disputes within the coalition must be reinforced, allowing them to act as an effective mediator between coalition partners and ensuring that minor disagreements do not escalate into full-blown government crises. In this regard, one possible reform is to give the prime minister greater authority over the appointment and dismissal of ministers. Currently, coalition partners often demand specific ministerial portfolios, which gives them leverage to destabilize the government if their demands are not met (see, for instance, the squabbles between Silvio Berlusconi and Giorgia Meloni over the appointment of Licia Ronzulli as minister of health in 2022). By giving the prime minister more discretion in appointing and removing ministers, the government can operate more efficiently and maintain greater cohesion. For example, in Germany the chancellor has considerable authority over the cabinet, which helps maintain discipline within coalition governments.

Another reform could involve streamlining the legislative process to reduce opportunities for coalition conflict. By simplifying procedures and clarifying the roles and responsibilities of coalition partners, the risk of disputes escalating into government-destabilizing conflicts can be minimized. For instance, formal rules could be introduced to limit the ability of coalition partners to block or delay key government initiatives, ensuring that the prime minister retains the authority to implement the government's legislative agenda.

The most relevant reform for the potential reduction of instability, however, is the adoption of the constructive vote of no confidence (see Section 2). Nevertheless, it must be noted that no single reform can fully resolve the problem of government instability in Italy – constitutional-engineering efforts cannot replace a culture of cooperation inherent in political parties. That is something that Italian political formations currently fail to develop. Nevertheless, I deem a combination of potentially useful reforms will foster greater stability, facilitating governments in conducting effective rule.

2 The role of the constructive vote of no confidence

One of the most relevant institutional mechanisms designed to mitigate government instability in parliamentary systems is the constructive vote of no confidence (henceforth, CVNC). This mechanism, introduced initially in post-World War II Germany, has since been adopted by a small number of democracies, particularly those characterized by multiparty, fragmented political systems and frequent government turnover. The CVNC requires that before a sitting government can be ousted, the opposition must agree on a new government ready to replace it. The primary goal of this instrument is to ensure that government changes occur in a predictable fashion, avoiding the possibility of a power vacuum.

Germany introduced the CVNC in 1949 under the Basic Law (*Grundgesetz*) as a direct response to the unstable governments formed during the Weimar Republic. Cabinets in that period were frequently brought down without any agreed-upon alternative, leading to a situation of political gridlock. The framers of the Basic Law thus sought to prevent such instability by ensuring that any motion of no confidence was accompanied by a viable alternative government.

After Germany, Spain adopted a similar provision in its 1978 constitution during its transition to democracy following Francisco Franco's authoritarian regime. Like Germany, Spain experienced significant social and political conflicts, and the constructive vote was interpreted as a tool to ensure stability in a fragmented system. Similarly, Belgium and Israel, two multiparty fragmented parliamentary democracies, introduced the CVNC in 1994 and 2001, respectively, as part of broader institutional reforms aimed at stabilizing coalition governments.

The stabilizing effect of the constructive vote of no confidence is that it deters opposition from unseating the government for opportunistic reasons. In systems without this mechanism, opposition parties can initiate no-confidence votes without any responsibility to propose a new government (a solution to the government crisis). This often leads to political paralysis or the formation of weak technocratic or caretaker cabinets, as Italy has observed during its various government crises. In contrast, the CVNC fosters greater responsibility among opposition parties (and members of the ruling majority seeking to defect), as they must negotiate and agree on a viable successor government before attempting to oust the incumbent one. For instance, in Germany the CVNC has reduced the number of no-confidence motions, as the requirement for an alternative executive discourages opposition parties from attempting to destabilize the government unless they are confident of garnering the necessary support for a successor. The same effect has been observed in Spain. In Belgium, the CVNC has played a role in stabilizing the country's highly fragmented system, yet it remains quite conflictual when it comes to coalition bargaining. Belgium's linguistic and cultural divisions have historically made it difficult for stable coalitions to form, but the introduction of the CVNC has made it harder for coalition partners to bring down the cabinet, albeit less so compared with other systems enacting the CVNC. Finally, in Israel the introduction of the CVNC in 2001 was part of a broader effort to stabilize the country's political system, which is characterized by many small parties and frequent government turnover due to the "politics of blocs" of the Israeli political system.

One of the key benefits of the CVNC in the Italian context would be to reduce the leverage of small parties within coalitions. Under the current system, small parties often hold disproportionate power within coalition governments, as they can threaten to withdraw their support and bring down the cabinet (see, for instance, Matteo Renzi's withdrawal of support in the Conte II cabinet). The CVNC would limit this behavior by making it harder for small parties to initiate no-confidence motions unless they could secure a majority for an alternative government. However, the introduction of the CVNC in Italy would not be without challenges. One potential drawback is that it could further entrench executive power, making it more difficult for parliament to hold the government to account. By raising the threshold for a no-confidence vote, the CVNC could reduce the ability of opposition parties to challenge the government, leading to an imbalance of power between the executive and the legislature. Moreover, in Italy's highly polarized political environment, it may be difficult for opposition parties to reach the necessary support to propose an alternative government, which could, again, lead to paralysis.

Given the potential benefits of the CVNC, yet considering also the potential drawbacks, Italy should consider introducing this mechanism to promote government stability. While the CVNC is not a panacea for all of Italy's political problems, it offers a solution to one of the country's long-standing issues. The CVNC could help Italy move towards a more stable parliamentary system.

Figure 6.1 confirms the stabilizing role of the CVNC, in line with previous studies (Improta, 2022a; Rubabshi-Shitrit & Hasson, 2023; Lento, 2023). The Kaplan–Meier survival curves comparing the two types of no-confidence motion (regular and constructive vote) document that the survival probability of the governments is significantly different: governments operating in a CVNC setting display a median survival rate higher than those ruling in a regular no-confidence framework.

In more detail, both curves show a steep decline in the survival probability at the beginning of the period studied (i.e., at the lower end of government duration).

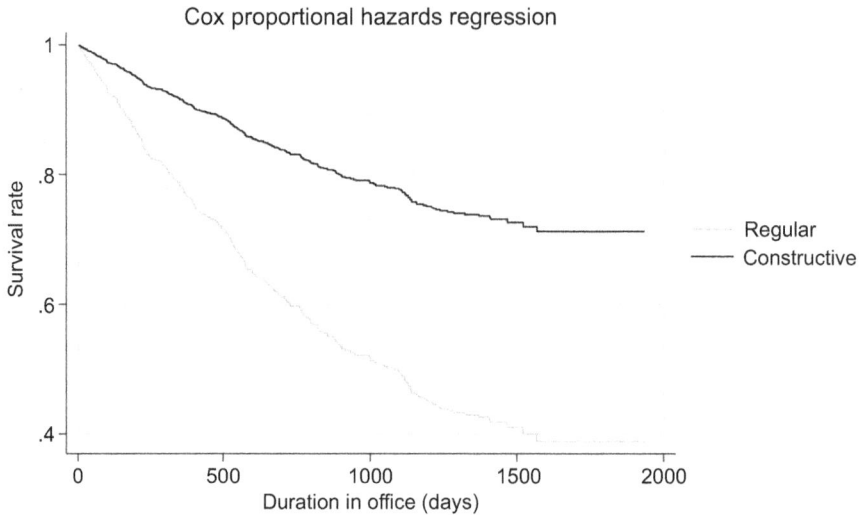

Figure 6.1: Cox regression of no-confidence vote.
Note: Cox analysis performed on the entire country sample.
Source: Own elaboration.

This suggests that regardless of whether a government is under the regular system or a CVNC system, there is a relatively high probability of government collapse within the first 500 days. This could indicate that many governments are vulnerable to termination shortly after formation. Regular motions in a specific government system consistently show a lower survival probability across the period compared with the CVNC system. This suggests that governments operating under the regular system have a higher probability of being terminated earlier. In contrast, governments operating under the CVNC system tend to survive longer, maintaining a higher survival probability throughout the period observed. The point where each curve drops below 0.5 survival probability indicates the median government duration. The regular motion reaches this point sooner than the CVNC, indicating that governments in the regular motion tend to collapse earlier. The CVNC shows a longer median survival time, which is consistent with the idea that the constructive vote of no-confidence mechanism helps prolong government stability by preventing termination. Beyond 1,500 days, both curves flatten, indicating that governments that survive this long are less likely to collapse immediately. However, the CVNC curve remains above the regular curve, meaning that governments under the CVNC system continue to have a higher probability of survival in the long term compared with regular governments.

Governments under the CVNC system tend to last longer, with fewer terminations occurring early in their tenure compared with those under regular systems. This suggests that the CVNC mechanism – by requiring a replacement government to be proposed before the current one is ousted – helps reduce the frequency of government collapse, ensuring a smoother and more stable governance process. Conversely, the regular system, which lacks such a safeguard, shows a higher likelihood of early government collapse.

3 Addressing the fragmentation problem: From electoral system to party discipline

The fragmentation of the Italian political system is a well-known phenomenon, which has attracted attention from generations of scholars. The issue became salient during the transition from the First to the Second Republic (for a review, see Chiaramonte & D'Alimonte, 2015), and is still crucial in the academic debate (Chiaramonte, 2024).

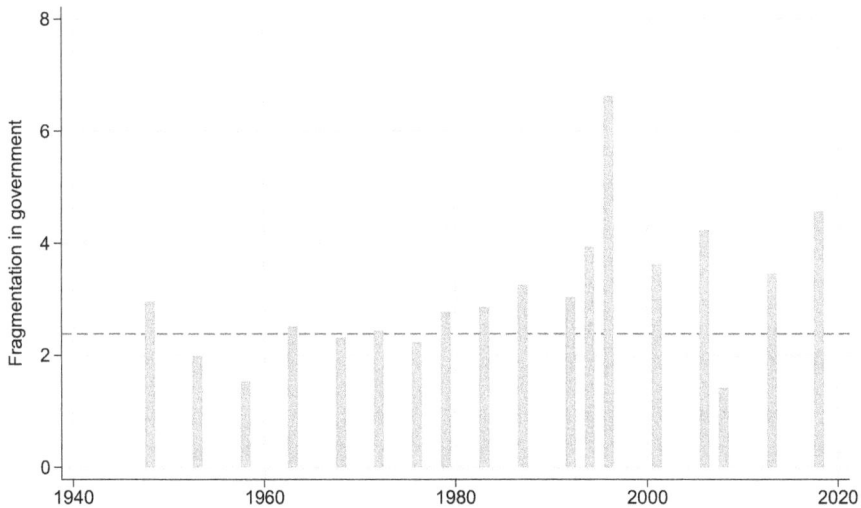

Figure 6.2: Fragmentation in government per decade.
Note: Vital supporting parties included.
Source: Own elaboration.

Figure 6.2 illustrates the severity of the fragmentation problem in Italy. The y-axis represents the level of government fragmentation, measured by the number of coalition parties, while the x-axis shows the years during which the governments were active. The black dashed line serves as a reference point, indicating the average level of fragmentation in the country across the period considered. We can observe that in the immediate post-war period, fragmentation appears to fluctuate, starting at a relatively high level in the late 1940s and early 1950s. The early democratic period in Italy was characterized by political instability, with multiple small parties participating in coalition governments. The graph shows that fragmentation levels remained relatively stable and close to the reference line through the late 1950s and early 1960s, reflecting a period where the dominant DC managed to maintain control, but still had to navigate coalition politics with several smaller parties. The 1970s and 1980s show a moderate increase in fragmentation. This rise can be attributed to the growing influence of DC's coalition partners, such as the PSI and other smaller parties (e.g., the Liberals). During this period, the relative stability of the party system gave way to more fragmented and contentious coalitions. Although the average level of fragmentation fluctuates, it does not surpass extreme levels during this period. Instead, fragmentation peaked dramatically towards the end of the 1990s, surpassing the reference line substantially. This period marks the decline of the traditional party system and the emergence of new political actors, leading to more complex and unstable coalition governments. Most recently, fragmentation has remained above the reference line.

How to solve the fragmentation problem? In this book, I maintain that in Italy it is crucial to adopt an approach that incorporates both electoral system reforms to address *entry fragmentation* and institutional measures to address *intra-legislature fragmentation*. Comparative constitutional engineering (Sartori, 1995b) offers a valuable framework for tackling this issue, as other democracies have successfully implemented reforms that reduce fragmentation and promote stability.

A primary cause of fragmentation in Italy stems from the electoral system. Proportional representation systems like Italy's tend to encourage the proliferation of small political formations, making more likely the development of transaction costs between coalition partners as well as ruling and opposition parties. While proportional representation systems allow for increased representation of different segments of society through parties (Lijphart, 1999), they can also lead to ineffective governance, especially when fragmentation becomes excessively high, creating fragile coalitions prone to internal conflict and premature end. One of the most effective potential solutions to address the entry fragmentation, namely the fragmentation created from the entry of parliamentary parties in the newly established legislature, is the introduction of high electoral thresholds. Many countries have adopted thresholds in their electoral systems to limit the entry of small parties, thereby encouraging the formation of more solid political blocs. A higher threshold requires parties to receive a minimum percentage of the vote (e.g., 5%) to gain representation in parliament. This of course reduces the number of small parties entering the legislature.

For example, Germany operates a mixed-member proportional representation system with a 5% electoral threshold, which has helped reduce fragmentation while still preserving a fair amount of proportionality. Germany's experience indicates that a well-calibrated threshold can limit the emergence of fragmentation without stifling political competition. However, there is a caveat to consider when discussing electoral thresholds. Turkey, for instance, imposes a 10% threshold. This is exceptionally high by democratic standards. Such thresholds are too exclusionary and should be applied to coalitions rather than single parties. In the Italian context, increasing the electoral threshold would be effective, and I propose a threshold of 5% for single parties.

Another potential solution to reduce fragmentation at the electoral stage is to introduce smaller constituencies or stronger majoritarian elements into the electoral system. Countries like France and the United Kingdom, albeit different in terms of democratic model, use majoritarian systems with single-member districts, which tend to favor larger parties and produce more stable governments (although, of course, there are circumstantial elements leading to exceptions). While Italy is unlikely to radically change democratic model and fully adopt a majoritarian system due to its consensus-based tradition, hybrid systems can be explored. For example, Italy could stress the elements of a mixed-member proportional system, similar to Germany's, where a portion of seats are filled through first-past-the-post single-member districts and the remainder are allocated proportionally. A move towards smaller constituencies would further reduce the influence of small formations.

While electoral system provisions are crucial for dealing with entry fragmentation, they are not sufficient to address the problem of intra-legislature fragmentation. Even after entering parliament, parties can fracture or exhibit poor discipline, with members of parliament deviating from the party line and rebelling. This often leads to government instability and government crises. Therefore, addressing the fragmentation emerging after the electoral and formation stage requires encouraging party discipline and discouraging defections. All that must be coupled with ensuring that such measures remain compatible with the Italian constitution and democratic principles (especially Article 67).

One possible reform is the introduction of anti-defection laws, which have been implemented in some other parliamentary democracies. These laws penalize members of parliament or political factions that deviate from the party line or split during their term, reducing the likelihood of coalition breakdowns. Anti-defection laws can prevent the destabilization of coalitions by making it more difficult for individual members of parliament to leave their party of election without consequences (Nikolenyi, 2023; Pinto, 2023). For instance, India has a well-known anti-defection law introduced in 1985, which aims to prevent parliamentarians from changing parties during the legislative term. According to this law, parliamentarians who defect from their party or vote against the party line on key issues face disqualification from their seat (Nikolenyi, 2019). This has helped reduce the frequency of government collapse.

However, India's experience should not be considered as the most preferred option, as it is too stringent and limits legitimate dissent within parties. For Italy, an anti-defection law would need to be carefully designed to comply with the guarantee of freedom of parliamentary representatives, who represent the whole Nation when elected as members of parliament, not just their party. Article 67 of the constitution explicitly states that parliamentarians exercise their functions without a binding mandate, meaning they are free to vote according to their conscience rather than their party affiliations. Any attempt to introduce anti-defection legislation must consider this constitutional provision. While the optimal solution would be enhancing a culture of cooperation within parties, other approaches could include, again, the formalization of coalition agreements. By formalizing coalition agreements, members of parliament would be more constrained when choosing to deviate from the agreed-upon policy goals.

In Italy, some attempts to solve the problem of party (in)discipline have been made by single parties (for instance, the M5S). These political formations have introduced a financial penalty for parliamentarians who leave the group due to political dissent. However, this provision has not produced the desired effects. On the one hand, the penalty has not significantly disincentivized defections by parliamentarians. On the other hand, the supremacy of the prohibition of the imperative mandates, as enshrined in Article 67, has served as an obstacle to collecting the established sum, repeatedly cited in the resolution of disputes that have arisen.

The ineffectiveness of the financial penalty was primarily due to the fact that this instrument was not placed within a broader institutional reform context that concerned all parliamentary political formations, but rather was limited to regulating the relationships between a specific party (e.g., the M5S) and the members of its parliamentary group. In light of this, alternative instruments that apply to the relationship between all parties and their parliamentary groups should be considered.

Given the ineffectiveness of the financial penalty, it is necessary to reflect on alternative instruments to protect parliamentary groups from the phenomenon of party-switching. There have been attempts in the recent past, of a bipartisan nature, although the main impetus has come from the proposals of the M5S. One proposal that, in my view, could potentially be revisited and reintroduced is as follows.

Constitutional Bill No. 2759, by first signatory Vito Crimi. The bill consists of a single article, aimed at amending Article 67 by establishing that "members of the Chamber of Deputies and Senators who, during the legislature, join a parliamentary group different from the one for which they were elected, shall be declared disqualified and ineligible." The bill was introduced in 2017 but was never discussed. This was clearly due to the M5S's status as an opposition group during the 17th legislature. Arguably, the provision of disqualification and ineligibility could be perceived by parliamentarians as too severe a penalty to endure. For this reason, it would be necessary to identify mitigating factors.

Following the example of Israel's anti-defection laws, a rewritten version of Bill No. 2759 should include two mitigating elements. First, parliamentarians who wish to leave their parliamentary group may do so within 180 days of the next election. Second, parliamentarians who wish to leave their group may do so if the defection involves at least one-third of the parliamentary group. The rationale behind the first element is that this provision protects the unity of the parliamentary group for a substantial period, allowing defections only close to the next electoral contest, a moment when party strategies are typically redefined in light of potential changes. The second element is designed to complicate the defection of an individual parliamentarian, who would need to seek broad consensus among other parliamentarians to leave the group. In this sense, the bill should be rewritten as follows:

> Every member of Parliament represents the Nation and exercises their functions with the binding mandate of the people. Members of the Chamber of Deputies and Senators who, during the legislature, join a parliamentary group different from the one to which they were elected shall be declared disqualified. Deputies and Senators may join a parliamentary group different from the one to which they were elected within 180 days of the next election or at any time if joining a parliamentary group different from the one to which they were elected involves at least one-third of the members of the parliamentary group.

Israel's anti-defection laws provide for a period of 90 days, not 180, according to the provisions of the Israeli Party Finance Law. However, in the Israeli legal system there is no prohibition of the imperative mandate, so it is appropriate, in the Italian case, to extend the period to 180 days.

All in all, this reform would mitigate the anti-defection laws proposed previously, as the binding mandate would be simply constrained by temporal factors and numerical (political) factors.

Conclusion

Analyzing government instability in Italy, I have highlighted the complex interplay between institutional design, fragmentation and coalition dynamics, and broader social factors. By tracing the evolution of Italy's instability across different "Republics," it is clear that government instability should be deemed a persistent challenge that has both deep historical (and institution-induced) roots and contemporary manifestations. Despite various reform attempts starting from the late 1970s aimed at stabilizing the executive branch (Improta & Marzi, 2024), the issue of government instability remains critical.

One of the key findings of this book is the significant role that party conflicts play in government instability. As demonstrated in the survival analysis presented in Chapter 5, the fragmentation in the governmental arena is a crucial predictor of early government termination. When coalitions are made up of a large number of political parties holding cabinet posts, the likelihood of government early collapse increases significantly. This is particularly evident in the First Republic, where the proliferation of small parties led to frequent government crises. In addition to fragmentation, the role of trust and perceived corruption emerged as significant factors in affecting survival in office. As hypothesized, governments operating in contexts where citizens have low trust in political parties are more vulnerable to early collapse. In a similar vein, high levels of perceived corruption erode the credibility of ruling coalitions and increase the likelihood of government termination.

The problem of instability is no news to policymakers. Some reforms were indeed introduced with the implicit objective of enhancing the stability of governments. I consider the reform attempts implicit in the sense that the aim was to amend the electoral system rather than explicitly alter provisions linked in a more direct fashion with government stability (e.g., the confidence procedure). The reforms introduced during the 1990s, particularly the shift towards a mixed-member electoral system, were intended to reduce fragmentation and promote the emergence of pre-electoral coalitions. However, while some minor improvements in stability can be recorded, the deeper, structural issues underpinning instability remained. The majoritarian elements of the new electoral system (Mattarella Law) encouraged the formation of a bipolar competition characterized by two larger political blocs, but the underlying problems of fragmentation and coalition conflicts remained.

Regarding reform attempts, at the time of this book's writing, the parliament is scrutinizing the Meloni–Casellati institutional reform proposal. As explained in

https://doi.org/10.1515/9783111329727-008

Improta and Marzi (2024), the institutional reform currently under consideration aims to radically alter the country's government system. The primary objectives of the reform include enhancing government stability and strengthening the link between voter preferences and government formation. However, these goals have been met with substantial criticism, especially concerning the proposed structural changes and their potential unintended consequences.

This reform aims to address government instability by introducing a direct election for the prime minister and a more explicit mechanism for forming and maintaining governments. Furthermore, the reform seeks to solidify the connection between the choices of the electorate and the formation of the government, thereby increasing election decisiveness. Another objective is to address fragmentation. In this regard, the reform aims to ensure that the elected prime minister has a clear mandate to govern without facing recurrent threats of collapse from coalition partners. In addition, the reform includes provisions to abolish life senators and modify the head of state's powers concerning parliament dissolution, both aimed at creating a less unpredictable political environment.

Despite these ambitious objectives and the proper identification of the instability problem, I believe the reform faces several critical challenges. One of the main concerns is the fact that this reform would introduce an unprecedented government system. Most importantly, it recalls the failed Israeli experiment of direct prime ministerial elections which took place between 1992 and 2001. However, it must be noted that there are critical differences between the two systems. If the reform were to be approved, we should hope for different outcomes compared with the Israeli ones. The Israeli case, indeed, shows that such reforms can lead to unintended consequences, such as increasing rather than reducing fragmentation, as voters may split their ballots between prime ministerial candidates and parliamentary candidates from different parties. While the Italian reform attempts to avoid this by introducing a majority bonus to ensure that the prime minister's affiliated party or coalition secures a solid majority of seats, the potential for similar issues to arise cannot be disregarded.

Another significant criticism relates to the proposed no-confidence mechanism. The reform introduces a peculiar system that seeks to maintain the elected prime minister's connection with voter preferences throughout the electoral cycle. However, the new (unprecedented) confidence mechanism, which allows the head of state to dissolve the parliament if the prime minister fails to secure confidence, raises concerns about the balance of power between the executive and the legislative branches. This mechanism limits the possibility of alternative parliamentary majorities forming during the legislature, potentially reducing the flexibility needed to address political crises and opposition concerns.

The reform's goal of government stability also faces skepticism, particularly regarding the potential for unintended consequences. Critics argue that the proposed changes could weaken the prime minister rather than strengthen them. For instance, the provision allowing a new prime minister to be appointed without triggering elections if the incumbent is removed might encourage internal divisions within the ruling majority, as parliamentarians may feel empowered to challenge the prime minister without risking electoral backlash. This scenario could paradoxically lead to greater instability, with frequent changes in leadership undermining the continuity and consistency of governance.

Moreover, the abolition of life senators, while intended to prevent their votes from influencing confidence votes, may not have the desired effect on government stability. Historically, life senators have played quite an important role in both government formation and termination, particularly in situations where narrow parliamentary majorities existed. By abolishing the figure of life senator in the institutional system of the country, the reform could inadvertently create more volatile parliamentary dynamics, where slim majorities are more susceptible to early collapse without the stabilizing influence of non-partisan life senators. Of course, I also see why proponents of the reform seek to eliminate the position of life senator. On some occasions, life senators have not observed non-partisan behavior, acting in a more politicized way, thus influencing political dynamics in the legislature. This may pose some concerns regarding democratic quality.

The Meloni–Casellati reform also opens up broader theoretical questions for political science, particularly in the field of institutional design and government systems. From a comparative perspective, the reform does not fit neatly into the traditional categories of presidential or parliamentary systems, instead proposing a hybrid model that combines elements of both. While the direct election of the prime minister is a hallmark of presidential systems, the retention of legislative confidence requirements maintains a key feature of parliamentary governance. This hybridization, while innovative, presents its own set of risks and uncertainties, particularly regarding how it will function in practice and whether it will achieve the intended outcomes.

Furthermore, the reform's focus on government stability raises questions about the role of rationalizing mechanisms in parliamentary systems, such as the constructive vote of no confidence. Countries like Germany, Belgium, and Spain have successfully implemented this mechanism to enhance government stability, and it has been discussed as a potential solution for Italy as well (Improta, 2022a).

However, the Meloni–Casellati reform takes a different approach, introducing a peculiar no-confidence mechanism that restricts the formation of alternative majorities, which may limit the flexibility of the parliamentary system and reduce its capacity to adapt to changing political conditions. Finally, the proposed reform's implications for political parties' behavior are profound. By limiting the opposition's ability to form alternative majorities during the legislative term, the reform could reduce the incentive for them to engage constructively in the legislative process. This, in turn, could lead to increased polarization and a more confrontational political environment, where the opposition's only viable strategy is to wait for the next election. Such an outcome could exacerbate existing tensions within the political system and further undermine the prospects for long-term stability.

The Meloni–Casellati reform is certainly a reform attempt that correctly identifies government instability as a problem for Italy, yet it also faces significant criticism. The lessons from Israel's failed experiment with direct prime ministerial elections serve as a cautionary tale, highlighting the potential for unintended consequences that could undermine the very objectives the reform seeks to achieve. Moreover, the reform's implications for parliamentary dynamics raise important questions that require careful consideration. Whether the reform succeeds in creating a more stable and effective government system will depend on several elements and it is still under question.

The book has highlighted the importance of institutional design in managing coalition conflicts. Italy, so far, has not fully implemented institutional safeguards against conflicts and instability. The absence of a constructive vote of no confidence, for instance, has made it easier for opposition parties to bring down governments without presenting viable alternatives, leading to frequent government crises.

The persistence of government instability in Italy raises important questions about the future of Italian democracy. While the reforms of the 1990s were a step in the right direction, more comprehensive changes are needed to address the root causes of instability. One potential solution is to further refine the electoral system, perhaps by introducing higher electoral thresholds to limit the number of small parties entering parliament. This would reduce the need for broad and often ideologically diverse coalitions, making it easier for governments to maintain internal cohesiveness and policy continuity. Additionally, addressing the issue of party discipline will be crucial for ensuring the long-term stability of Italian governments. The introduction of formal coalition agreements – as seen in countries like Germany – could help prevent internal conflicts by binding parties to a shared policy agenda. Such agreements would reduce the likelihood of defections and ensure that coalition partners remain committed to their government's survival, even in the face of external challenges. Of course, the broader political context also plays a role when it comes to government instability. As this book has shown, low levels of trust in political parties and high levels of corruption exacerbate the fragility of Italian governments. Therefore, efforts to improve transparency, accountability, and public trust in political institutions will be essential for reducing the risk of government collapse, as well as other important dimensions of democratic quality. This will require not only institutional reforms but also a concerted effort to rebuild the relationship between political parties and voters.

Looking ahead, there are several key recommendations for addressing the problem of government instability in Italy. First, as mentioned, introducing higher electoral thresholds would reduce fragmentation by limiting the number of small parties and encouraging the formation of coalitions that are not "oversized." Second is the implementation of anti-defection laws. In this regard, by preventing parliamentarians from switching party mid-term, these laws would help maintain the integrity of coalition governments and reduce internal conflicts. Third, we should think about the strengthening of coalition agreements. Requiring coalition partners to commit to formal agreements outlining shared policy goals would help prevent internal divisions and ensure that governments survive longer. Fourth, there is a need to improve transparency and accountability: reducing corruption and improving public trust in parties would be achieved by introducing anti-corruption measures. This is not an easy task, of course, but it is much needed in a country like Italy. Finally, and most importantly, Italy could think about introducing the constructive vote of no confidence.

By implementing these reforms, Italy could try to address the persistent instability and move towards a more stable and effective political system. The recommendations outlined above aim to tackle both the institutional weaknesses that have plagued Italian governance and the broader political and social factors that exacerbate instability.

The road ahead for Italy's political system requires a careful balance between institutional engineering and fostering a political culture that values long-term governance over short-term political gains. As the book has shown, no single reform alone will be sufficient to fully address the issue of government instability. Rather, a combination of measures, both institutional and social, will be needed to ensure that Italian governments can survive long enough to implement meaningful policies that address the needs of their citizens. The so-called "Third Republic," which has seen the rise of new political actors and continued electoral vola-tility, represents both a challenge and an opportunity for Italy's democracy. The rise of challenger parties and the weakening of mainstream formations have cre-ated novel uncertainties, but also an opportunity for political renewal. If Italy can successfully implement the suggested reforms, it has the potential to transform its political system into one that is more stable, transparent, and responsive.

Ultimately, the success of the reforms will depend on the willingness of Italy's po-litical leaders to embrace change and work towards a more stable political future. By learning from its own history and the experiences of other democracies, Italy can take the necessary steps to address its long-standing problem of government instability and build a stronger democracy.

References

Adams, J. C., & Barile, P. (1953). The implementation of the Italian Constitution. *American Political Science Review, 47*(1), 61–83.

Alesina, A., Michalopoulos, S., & Papaioannou, E. (2016). Ethnic inequality. *Journal of Political Economy, 124*(2), 428–488.

Allum, P. A. (1974). Italy – Republic without government? *The World Today, 30*(11), 448–459.

Angelucci, D., Improta, M., Lachat, R., & Vittori, D. (2024). Time will tear us apart: European electoral participation dynamics in longitudinal perspective. *Electoral Studies, 90*, 102819.

Angelucci, D., Improta, M., & Mannoni, E. (2024). Government instability and support for the political system. Paper presented at the SISP Conference, University of Trieste, Italy.

Baldini, G. (2017). La lunga e tormentata storia delle riforme istituzionali in Italia: Perché anche Renzi ha fallito. In A. Pritoni, M. Valbruzzi, & R. Vignati (Eds.), *La prova del No: Il sistema politico italiano dopo il referendum costituzionale* (pp. 11–26). Rubbettino.

Battegazzorre, F. (1987). L'instabilità di governo in Italia. *Italian Political Science Review/Rivista Italiana di Scienza Politica, 17*(2), 285–317.

Bergman, T., Bäck, H., & Hellström, J. (2021). The three stages of the coalition life cycle. In R. Y. Hazan & B. E. Rasch (Eds.). *Coalition governance in Western Europe* (pp. 15–40). Oxford University Press.

Bertsou, E. (2019). Rethinking political distrust. *European Political Science Review, 11*(2), 213–230.

Blossfeld, H. P., Rohwer, G., Schneider, T., & Halpin, B. (2019). *Event history analysis with Stata.* Routledge.

Browne, E. C., Frendreis, J. P., & Gleiber, D. W. (1984). An "events" approach to the problem of cabinet stability. *Comparative Political Studies, 17*(2), 167–197.

Calise, M. (2015). *Government and prime minister.* Oxford University Press.

Capati, A., Improta, M., & Lento, T. (2023). Ruling in turbulent times: Government crises in Italy and Israel during the COVID-19 pandemic. *Frontiers in Political Science, 5*, 1151288.

Carey, J. M., & Shugart, M. S. (1995). Incentives to cultivate a personal vote: A rank ordering of electoral formulas. *Electoral Studies, 14*(4), 417–439.

Chiaramonte, A. (2024). Quale sistema elettorale per il premierato? Dilemmi e prospettive. *Osservatorio sulle fonti, 2024*, 1–17.

Chiaramonte, A., & D'Alimonte, R. (2015). The field of electoral systems research in international and Italian political science. *Italian Political Science, 10*(1), 1–8.

Chiaramonte, A., & Emanuele, V. (2013). Volatile e tripolare: Il nuovo sistema partitico italiano. In L. De Sio, M. Cataldi, & F. De Lucia (Eds.), *Le elezioni politiche 2013* (pp. 95–100). Dossier CISE 4.

Chiaramonte, A., & Emanuele, V. (2022). *The deinstitutionalization of Western European party systems.* Palgrave Macmillan.

Cioffi-Revilla, C. (1984). The political reliability of Italian governments: An exponential survival model. *American Political Science Review, 78*(2), 318–337.

Clark, M. (2013). *The Italian Risorgimento.* Routledge.

Coppedge, M., Gerring, J., Knutsen, C. H., Lindberg, S. I., Teorell, J., Altman, D., . . . & Ziblatt, D. (2021). *V-Dem codebook v11.* https://doi.org/10.23696/vdemds21.

Cotta, M., & Marangoni, F. (2015). *Il governo.* Il Mulino.

Cotta, M., & Verzichelli, L. (2007). *Political institutions in Italy.* Oxford University Press.

Curini, L., & Pinto, L. (2017). *L'arte di fare (e disfare) i governi: Da De Gasperi a Renzi, 70 anni di politica italiana.* EGEA spa.

https://doi.org/10.1515/9783111329727-009

D'Alimonte, R. (2005). Italy: A case of fragmented bipolarism. In M. Gallagher & P. Mitchell (Eds.), *The politics of electoral systems* (pp. 253–276). Oxford University Press.

D'Alimonte, R., & Mammarella, G. (2022). *L'Italia della svolta: 2011–2021*. Il Mulino.

Damgaard, E. (2008). Cabinet termination in Western Europe. In K. W. Strøm, W. C. Müller, & T. Bergman (Eds.), *Cabinets and coalition bargaining: The democratic life cycle in Western Europe* (pp. 301–326). Oxford University Press.

Dassonneville, R., & McAllister, I. (2020). The party choice set and satisfaction with democracy. *West European Politics*, *43*(1), 49–73.

De Angelis, A., & Vecchiato, A. (2024). Panem et circenses: Removing political news to generate electoral support, evidence from Berlusconi's Italy. *Italian Political Science Review/Rivista Italiana di Scienza Politica*, aop1–19.

Diamanti, I. (2009). *Mappe dell'Italia politica: Bianco, rosso, verde, azzurro ... e tricolore*. Il Mulino.

Diamond, L., & Morlino, L. (2004). The quality of democracy: An overview. *Journal of Democracy*, *15*(4), 20–31.

Elgie, R. (2011). Semi-presidentialism in Western Europe. In R. Elgie, S. Moestrup, & W. Yu-Shan (Eds.), *Semi-Presidentialism and democracy* (pp. 81–97). Palgrave Macmillan.

Emanuele, V., Improta, M., Marino, B., & Verzichelli, L. (2023). Going technocratic? Diluting governing responsibility in electorally turbulent times. *West European Politics*, *46*(5), 995–1023.

Fabbrini, S., & Piattoni, S. (Eds.) (2008). *Italy in the European Union: Redefining national interest in a compound polity*. Rowman & Littlefield.

Fittipaldi, R., & Musella, F. (2022). Duration and durability of the Italian Governments: An old paradox revisited. *Italian Political Science*, *17*(2), 121–137.

Franco, D. (2002). Italy: A never-ending pension reform. In M. Feldstein & H. Siebert (Eds.), *Social security pension reform in Europe* (pp. 211–262). University of Chicago Press.

Franco, D., & Tommasino, P. (2020). Lessons from Italy: A good pension system needs an effective broader social policy framework. *Intereconomics*, *55*(2), 73–81.

Franklin, M. N., & Mackie, T. T. (1984). Reassessing the importance of size and ideology for the formation of governing coalitions in parliamentary democracies. *American Journal of Political Science*, *28*(4), 671–692.

Garmann, S. (2017). Election frequency, choice fatigue, and voter turnout. *European Journal of Political Economy*, *47*, 19–35.

Gentile, E. (2013). *Fascismo: Storia e interpretazione*. Gius.Laterza.

Ginsborg, P. (2005). *Silvio Berlusconi: Television, power and patrimony*. Verso.

Huber, J. D. (1998). How does cabinet instability affect political performance? Portfolio volatility and health care cost containment in parliamentary democracies. *American Political Science Review*, *92*(3), 577–591.

Ignazi, P. (1989). *Il polo escluso: Profilo del Movimento Sociale Italiano*. Il Mulino.

Improta, M. (2021). Inside technocracy: Features and trajectories of technocratic ministers in Italy (1948–2021). *Italian Political Science*, *16*(3), 220–240.

Improta, M. (2022a). L'elisir di lunga vita? Sfiducia costruttiva e stabilità dei governi in prospettiva comparata. *Rivista Italiana di Politiche Pubbliche*, *17*(2), 269–297.

Improta, M. (2022b). Unpacking government instability: Cabinet duration, innovation, and termination events in Italy between 1948 and 2021. *Quaderni di scienza politica*, *29*(2), 151–180.

Improta, M. (2023). *"Staying alive": The patterns and dynamics of government stability in 21 democracies (1945–2021)*. PhD Dissertation. LUISS Rome.

Improta, M. (2024). Paralysed governments: How political constraints elicit cabinet termination. *Parliamentary Affairs*, *77*(3), 470–488.

Improta, M., & Mannoni, E. (2024). Government short-termism and the management of global challenges. *British Journal of Politics and International Relations*, 13691481241280172.

Improta, M., & Marzi, P. (2024). The Meloni–Casellati institutional reform: Towards a new government system? *International Journal of Parliamentary Studies*, *1*(aop), 1–21.

Indridason, I. H., & Kam, C. (2008). Cabinet reshuffles and ministerial drift. *British Journal of Political Science*, *38*(4), 621–656.

King, G., Alt, J. E., Burns, N. E., & Laver, M. (1990). A unified model of cabinet dissolution in parliamentary democracies. *American Journal of Political Science*, *34*, 846–871.

Klüver, H., Bäck, H., & Krauss, S. (2023). *Coalition agreements as control devices: Coalition governance in Western and Eastern Europe*. Oxford University Press.

Körner, A. (2009). The Risorgimento's literary canon and the aesthetics of reception: Some methodological considerations. *Nations & Nationalism*, *15*(3), 410–418.

Laakso, M., & Taagepera, R. (1979). "Effective" number of parties: A measure with application to West Europe. *Comparative Political Studies*, *12*(1), 3–27.

Lento, T. (2023). Adopting the constructive vote of no-confidence: Belgium and Israel in comparative perspective. *International Journal of Parliamentary Studies*, *1*(aop), 1–26.

Lento, T., & Hazan, R. Y. (2023). The vote of no confidence: Towards a framework for analysis. In R. Y. Hazan & B. E. Rasch (Eds.), *Parliaments and government termination* (pp. 47–71). Routledge.

Lijphart, A. (1984). Measures of cabinet durability: A conceptual and empirical evaluation. *Comparative Political Studies*, *17*(2), 265–279.

Lijphart, A. (1999). *Patterns of democracy: Government forms and performance in thirty-six countries*. Yale University Press.

Lowell, A. L. (1896). *Governments and parties in Continental Europe. Volume II*. Harvard University Press.

Mack Smith, D. (1988). *The making of Italy, 1796–1866*. Springer.

Mack Smith, D. (1997). *Storia d'Italia dal 1861 al 1997*. Laterza.

Mair, P. (2009). *Representative versus responsible government*. Max-Planck-Institute.

Marangoni, F. (2012). Technocrats in government: The composition and legislative initiatives of the Monti government eight months into its term of office. *Bulletin of Italian Politics*, *4*(1), 135–149.

Marangoni, F., & Kreppel, A. (2022). From the "yellow-red" to the technocratic government in the pandemic era: The formation and activity of the Draghi government during its first nine months in charge. *Contemporary Italian Politics*, *14*(2), 133–150.

Martelli, P. (2018). *L'istituzione del disordine: Regole del gioco e giocatori nella politica italiana dal 1946 al 2018*. Rubbettino.

Mershon, C. (1996). The costs of coalition: Coalition theories and Italian governments. *American Political Science Review*, *90*(3), 534–554.

Morlino, L. (2011). *Changes for democracy: Actors, structures, processes*. Oxford University Press.

Müller, W. C., Strøm, K., & Bergman, T. (2008). Coalition theory and cabinet governance: An introduction. In K. Strøm, W. C. Müller, & T. Bergman (Eds.), *Cabinets and coalition bargaining: The democratic life cycle in Western Europe* (pp. 1–50). Oxford University Press.

Müller, W. C., & Strøm, K. (2000). Coalition governance in Western Europe: An introduction. *Coalition Governments in Western Europe*, *1*(1), 1–32.

Neuberger, B. (2020). Israel's unstable democracy in comparative perspective. *Israel Affairs*, *26*(6), 833–853.

Nikolenyi, C. (2019). Changing patterns of party unity in the Knesset: The consequences of the Israeli anti-defection law. *Party Politics*, *25*(5), 712–723.

Nikolenyi, C. (2023). Government termination and anti-defection laws in parliamentary democracies. In R. Y. Hazan & B. E. Rasch (Eds.), *Parliaments and government termination* (pp. 183–207). Routledge.

Nordhaus, W. D. (1975). The political business cycle. *Review of Economic Studies, 42*(2), 169–190.

Pasquino, G. (2023). *Nuovo corso di scienza politica*. Il Mulino.

Penati, C. (2015). The hearth of our times: Rai and the domestication of Italian television in the 1950s. *Comunicazioni Sociali, 1,* 36–45.

Pinto, L. (2023). Anti-defection rules and party switching in the Italian Parliament. *Party Politics,* 13540688231204310.

Pombeni, P. (2016). *La questione costituzionale in Italia*. Il Mulino.

Powell Jr., G. B. (2004). The quality of democracy: The chain of responsiveness. *Journal of Democracy, 15*(4), 91–105.

Rahat, G., & Hazan, R. Y. (2022). The political system and political parties. In G. Ben-Porat, Y. Feniger, D. Filc, P. Kabalo, & J. Mirsky (Eds.), *Routledge handbook on contemporary Israel* (pp. 75–87). Routledge. https://www.taylorfrancis.com/chapters/edit/10.4324/9780429281013-9/political-system-political-parties-gideon-rahat-reuven-hazan.

Riall, L. (2002). *The Italian Risorgimento: State, society and national unification*. Routledge.

Riker, W. H. (1962). *The theory of political coalitions*. Yale University Press.

Rubabshi-Shitrit, A., & Hasson, S. (2023). The effect of the constructive vote of no-confidence on government termination and government durability. In R. Y. Hazan & B. E. Rasch (Eds.), *Parliaments and government termination* (pp. 121–135). Routledge.

Saalfeld, T. (2008). Institutions, chance and choices: The dynamics of cabinet survival. In K. Strøm, W. C. Müller, & T. Bergman (Eds.), *Cabinet governance: Bargaining and the cycle of democratic politics* (pp. 327–368). Oxford University Press.

Sani, G. (1973). La strategia del PCI e l'elettorato italiano. *Italian Political Science Review/Rivista Italiana di Scienza Politica, 3*(3), 551–579.

Santagata, A. (2014). Ruinismo: The Catholic Church in Italy from "mediation culture" to the Cultural Project. *Journal of Modern Italian Studies, 19*(4), 438–452.

Sartori, G. (1976). *Parties and party systems: Volume 1: A framework for analysis*. Cambridge University Press.

Sartori, G. (1982). *Teoria dei partiti e caso italiano*. SugarCo.

Sartori, G. (1991). Comparing and miscomparing. *Journal of Theoretical Politics, 3*(3), 243–257.

Sartori, G. (1995a). Elogio del semi-presidenzialismo. *Italian Political Science Review/Rivista Italiana di Scienza Politica, 25*(1), 3–20.

Sartori, G. (1995b). How far can free government travel? *Journal of Democracy, 6*(3), 101–111.

Shamir, M., & Rahat, G. (Eds.) (2022). *The elections in Israel, 2019–2021*. Taylor & Francis.

Shomer, Y., Rasch, B. E., & Akirav, O. (2023). Open access: Termination of parliamentary governments: Revised definitions and implications. In R. Y. Hazan & B. E. Rasch (Eds.), *Parliaments and government termination* (pp. 95–120). Routledge.

Siaroff, A. (2003). Comparative presidencies: The inadequacy of the presidential, semi-presidential and parliamentary distinction. *European Journal of Political Research, 42*(3), 287–312.

Strøm, K., Bergman, T., Müller, W. C., & Nyblade, B. (2008). Conclusion: Cabinet governance in parliamentary democracies. In K. Strøm, W. C. Müller, & T. Bergman (Eds.), *Cabinets and coalition bargaining: The democratic life cycle in Western Europe* (pp. 403–430). Oxford University Press.

Tarchi, M. (1998). The Lega Nord. In L. De Winter & H. Tursan (Eds.), *Regionalist parties in Western Europe* (pp. 143–157). Routledge.

Tsebelis, G. (1995). Decision making in political systems: Veto players in presidentialism, parliamentarism, multicameralism and multipartyism. *British Journal of Political Science, 25*(3), 289–325.

Van Biezen, I., Mair, P., & Poguntke, T. (2012). Going, going, ... gone? The decline of party membership in contemporary Europe. *European Journal of Political Research, 51*(1), 24–56.

Verzichelli, L., & Cotta, M. (2018). Shades of technocracy: The variable use of non-partisan ministers in Italy. In A. Costa Pinto, M. Cotta, & P. Tavares de Almeida (Eds.), *Technocratic ministers and political leadership in European democracies* (pp. 77–110). Palgrave.

Wanrooij, B. (1987). The rise and fall of Italian fascism as a generational revolt. *Journal of Contemporary History, 22*(3), 401–418.

Warwick, P. (1994). *Government survival in parliamentary democracies*. Cambridge University Press.

Zamagni, V. (1993). *The economic history of Italy 1860–1990*. Clarendon Press.

Zucchini, F., & Pedrazzani, A. (2021). Italy: Continuous change and continuity in change. In T. Bergman, H. Bäck, & J. Hellström (Eds.), *Coalition governance in Western Europe* (pp. 396–447). Oxford University Press.

Appendix: Data codebook

This section presents the codebook of the original dataset that has been used for this book.

1 Description

The Dataset of Governments in 21 Western Democracies provides data on governments in 21 democracies since 1945. Data for Cyprus, Greece, Portugal, and Spain (the so-called "late democratization" countries) have been collected since the 1970s. Currently, the dataset includes more than 700 governments and is structured on three levels: country, election, and cabinet.

2 Content

1. Country: Name of the country in alphabetical order (Austria, Belgium, Cyprus, Denmark, Finland, France, Germany, Greece, Iceland, Ireland, Israel, Italy, Luxembourg, Malta, Netherlands, Norway, Portugal, Spain, Sweden, Switzerland, UK).

2. CountryCab: Cabinet number for each country.

3. Name: Name of the prime minister.

4. Start: Start date of the government.

5. End: End date of the government.

6. Duration: Government duration in days.

7. Legislature: Government legislature.

8. Composition: Party composition of the government.

9. PrimeMinister: Party of the prime minister.

10. NonPartisanCabinet: Dichotomous variable coded as "0" if the government is led by a party member prime minister, and "1" if the prime minister is non-partisan (e.g., technocrat, caretaker, expert, or independent).

11. NCabinetParties: Number of parties holding offices in the government.

https://doi.org/10.1515/9783111329727-010

12. TotalNumberOfMinistries: Total number of ministries; if a minister or the prime minister holds more than one ministerial office, they are counted as one person (e.g., Corrado Passera in the Monti government, Italy).

13. IndependentMinister: Number of ministers not belonging to a party.

14. FirstParty: Name of the party holding the majority of ministerial offices.

15. FirstP_N: Number of ministerial offices held by the first party.

16. SecondParty: Name of the second party in terms of ministerial offices.

17. SecondP_N: Number of ministerial offices held by the second party.

18. ThirdParty: Name of the third party in terms of ministerial offices.

19. ThirdP_N: Number of ministerial offices held by the third party.

20. FourthParty: Name of the fourth party in terms of ministerial offices.

21. FourthP_N: Number of ministerial offices held by the fourth party.

22. FifthParty: Name of the fifth party in terms of ministerial offices.

23. FifthP_N: Number of ministerial offices held by the fifth party.

24. SixthParty: Name of the sixth party in terms of ministerial offices.

25. SixthP_N: Number of ministerial offices held by the sixth party.

26. SeventhParty: Name of the seventh party in terms of ministerial offices.

27. SeventhP_N: Number of ministerial offices held by the seventh party.

28. EighthParty: Name of the eighth party in terms of ministerial offices.

29. EighthP_N: Number of ministerial offices held by the eighth party.

30. NinthParty: Name of the ninth party in terms of ministerial offices.

31. NinthP_N: Number of ministerial offices held by the ninth party.

32. TenthParty: Name of the tenth party in terms of ministerial offices.

33. TenthP_N: Number of ministerial offices held by the tenth party.

34. IdeologicalPosition: Ideological position based on the left–right dimension; coded as follows:
- 0 = left
- 1 = center-left
- 2 = center

- 3 = center-right
- 4 = right.

35. GoverningFormula: Dichotomous variable coded "0" if the governing formula is familiar (the government is led by parties that have previously governed together or is a single-party majority that has governed before). "1" indicates an innovative governing formula, meaning the government could be composed of:
- a single party that has never governed
- a coalition that has never governed
- a coalition including a party that has never governed
- a coalition including parties that have never governed together.

36. TypeOfGovernment: Type of government coded as follows:
- 0 = multiparty minority government
- 1 = single-party minority government
- 2 = oversized majority government
- 3 = minimum winning coalition
- 4 = single-party majority government.

This follows the main theories in political coalition studies (mainly Riker, 1962).

37. ParliamentarySeats: Percentage of seats in parliament held by the government; the representative assemblies considered are the lower house in cases of bicameralism.

38. EffectiveNumberOfParties: Effective number of government parties, based on Laakso and Taagepera's (1979) formula for effective electoral parties.

39. ConfidenceVote: Dichotomous variable, where "1" indicates an explicit vote of confidence and "0" indicates an implicit vote, meaning it is not constitutionally required for a new government.

40. Confidence_Dum: Constructive vote of no confidence based on Lento and Hazan (2023).
- 0 = regular vote of no confidence
- 1 = constructive vote of no confidence

41. Formula2: Similar to GoverningFormula, but also considers changes in the balance of power among coalition parties as reasons for innovative governing formulas.

42. Left: Dichotomous variable coded "0" if there are no left parties in government, "1" if there are left parties in government.

43. LeftPM: Dichotomous variable coded "0" if the prime minister does not belong to a left party, "1" if they do.

44. LeftWeight: Weight of the left within the government, operationalized as a percentage: (number of ministers belonging to a left party / total number of ministers) * 100.

45. Incumbent: Dichotomous variable, coded "1" if the prime minister of the previous legislature opens the next legislature, "0" otherwise.

46. LastGov: Dichotomous variable, where "1" indicates the government is the last of the legislature and "0" otherwise.

47. Cntry: Number associated with each country (e.g., 11 = Italy).

48. Cabinet_N: Number of the government across the entire dataset.

49. DumCount1: Dummy variable, where "1" indicates that the country considered is Austria.

50. DumCount2: Dummy variable, where "1" indicates that the country considered is Belgium.

51. DumCount3: Dummy variable, where "1" indicates that the country considered is Cyprus.

52. DumCount4: Dummy variable, where "1" indicates that the country considered is Denmark.

53. DumCount5: Dummy variable, where "1" indicates that the country considered is Finland.

54. DumCount6: Dummy variable, where "1" indicates that the country considered is France.

55. DumCount7: Dummy variable, where "1" indicates that the country considered is Germany.

56. DumCount8: Dummy variable, where "1" indicates that the country considered is Greece.

57. DumCount9: Dummy variable, where "1" indicates that the country considered is Iceland.

58. DumCount10: Dummy variable, where "1" indicates that the country considered is Ireland.

59. DumCount11: Dummy variable, where "1" indicates that the country considered is Italy.

60. DumCount12: Dummy variable, where "1" indicates that the country considered is Luxembourg.

61. DumCount13: Dummy variable, where "1" indicates that the country considered is Malta.

62. DumCount14: Dummy variable, where "1" indicates that the country considered is the Netherlands.

63. DumCount15: Dummy variable, where "1" indicates that the country considered is Norway.

64. DumCount16: Dummy variable, where "1" indicates that the country considered is Portugal.

65. DumCount17: Dummy variable, where "1" indicates that the country considered is Spain.

66. DumCount18: Dummy variable, where "1" indicates that the country considered is Sweden.

67. DumCount19: Dummy variable, where "1" indicates that the country considered is Switzerland.

68. DumCount20: Dummy variable, where "1" indicates that the country considered is the United Kingdom.

69. Start_Year: Start year of the government.

70. Decade: Decade in which the government was formed (e.g., 1940s, 1950s, 1960s).

71. Country_Short: Abbreviation of the country name (e.g., Austria = AT).

72. Left_Gov: Dichotomous variable coded "0" if the government does not contain a left party, "1" if it does.

73. Year: Start year of the legislature.

74. Election_Date: Exact date of the election.

75. RegV: Internal component of electoral volatility, disaggregation of Pedersen's index of aggregate volatility; regeneration volatility is the volatility derived from a new party entry and an old party exit.

76. AltV: Internal component of electoral volatility, disaggregation of Pedersen's index of aggregate volatility; alteration volatility is the volatility derived from switches among existing parties.

77. OthV: Volatility of parties below 1% in both time1 and time2.

78. TV: Total volatility in the party system (RegV + AltV + OthV).

79. RegPV: Proportional volatility due to regeneration.

80. AltPV: Proportional volatility due to alteration.

81. OthPV: Proportional volatility due to other parties.

82. TPV: Total proportional volatility.

83. PSINN: Percentage of new parties in the parliament.

84. CPSINN: Cumulative percentage of new parties.

85. Parl_INN: Percentage of parliamentary innovations.

86. GALT: Left–right polarization score (green–alternative–libertarian vs. traditionalist–authoritarian–nationalist).

87. GINN: Percentage of governing parties that are new.

88. Multi_Min: Dichotomous variable, where "1" indicates a multiparty minority government.

89. Mono_Min: Dichotomous variable, where "1" indicates a single-party minority government.

90. Oversized: Dichotomous variable, where "1" indicates an oversized majority government.

91. Min_Winn: Dichotomous variable, where "1" indicates a minimum winning coalition.

92. Mono_Maj: Dichotomous variable, where "1" indicates a single-party majority government.

93. Technici_Pct: Percentage of technocratic ministers in the government (number of technocratic ministers / total number of ministerial offices * 100).

94. FirstGov: Dichotomous variable, where "1" indicates the government is the first of the legislature and "0" otherwise.

95. PolarDalton: Polarization score based on Dalton's index.

96. Polar_Weighted: Weighted polarization index.

97. ENEP: Effective number of electoral parties.

98. Dispr: Disproportionality index of the electoral system.

99. MDM: Measure of median voter distance.

100. Ln_MDM: Logarithmic transformation of MDM.

101. Turnout: Voter turnout percentage.

102. Turn_Diff: Difference in voter turnout between elections.

103. Turnout_Change: Percentage change in voter turnout.

104. IPELF: Index of polarization in electoral and legislative fields.

105. BirthYear: Year of formation of the political party.

106. Age_Dem: Age of democracy in years.

107. Alesina: Index based on Alesina et al.'s (2016) model.

108. TimBetElec: Time between elections.

109. GDP_Rate: One-year lagged GDP growth rate.

110. Unemployment_Rate: One-year lagged unemployment rate.

111. Gro_Coal: Dichotomous variable, "1" if mainstream parties govern together.

112. Ginn_Gov: Percentage of new parties in government.

113. First_Alt: Dichotomous variable indicating first alternation in government.

114. Election: Numerical listing of elections for all countries.

115. Formula_Pura: Pure formula coding.

116. Cabinet: Specific cabinet identifier.

117. Cab_Count: Number of cabinets per legislature.

118. ENOP: Effective number of opposition parties.

119. POP: Permanent opposition presence.

120. Left_Right: Cabinet's party composition based on left–right classification.

121. Polar_Votes and Polar_Seats: Polarization in electoral and parliamentary arenas.

122. Barg_Dur: Duration of the bargaining process in days.

123. Personal_Vote: Measure based on Carey and Shugart (1995).

124. Semi_Presidentialism: Classification following Elgie's (2011) dataset.

125. Presidential_Powers: Scoring of presidential powers (Siaroff, 2003).

126. Lijphart: Classification variable; 0 = consensus, 1 = intermediate, 2 = Westminster.

127. DemWgt: Percentage of demarcation parties within government.

128. Gfce: One-year lagged government consumption expenditure.

129. GovDebt: One-year lagged general government debt as % of GDP.

130. Termination: Cabinet termination indicator (0 = elections, 1 = replacement).

131. EuroSud: Southern European country indicator.

132. Survival: Survival rate of the cabinet.

133. GeogArea: Geographic classification (e.g., Southern, Northern).

134. VoteOfConfidence: Categorization of confidence vote restrictiveness.

135. Government_Opposition_Volatility: Measure of volatility between government and opposition.

136. Coal_Agreement: Classification of coalition agreements.

137. NonTechIndMin_Abs: Number of non-technical independent ministers.

138. NonTechIndMin_Misplaced: Misplaced independent ministers count.

139. NonTechIndMin_NoCompetence: Count of independent ministers without competence.

140. Technocrat_Led: Indicator of technocratic PMs.

141. EU_Membership: EU membership indicator based on year.

142. Troika: Dummy variable indicating agreement with the Troika.

143. Euro: Classification for Eurozone membership.

144. Trust_Parties: Trust in parties based on Eurobarometer.

145. Scandal: Indicator of scandal occurrence before government formation.

146. Corruption: Corruption indicator based on start year.

147. ElectoralSystem: Classification of the electoral system.

148. Min_Experience: Percentage of experienced ministers.

149. Returnability: Share of parties returning to power.

Index

Note: Page numbers in *italics* indicate figures, and page numbers in **bold** indicate tables in the text

Albertine Statute 15
Allum, P. A. 9
Amendola, G. 25
Angelucci, D. 9
anti-defection laws 78–80
anti-fascist resistance 18

Battegazzorre, F. 30, 31
Bennett, N. 5
Berlusconi, S. 2, 19
– Berlusconi IV 44
– governments 58
Blanch, L. 16
Brothers of Italy 60

cabinet terminations 5–6, 8, 11–12
– causes of **39–43**, 45, 63–64
Calamandrei, P. 24
Calise, M. 27
Christian Democracy (DC) 1, 17, 20
codebook for government dataset 93–101
comparative constitutional engineering 76
confidence mechanism 82
consensus democracies 5, 10
Constitutional Court 25
constructive vote of no confidence (CVNC) 71
– benefits of 73
– Cox regression *74*
– enhanced government stability 75
– government survival and impact of 74
– Kaplan–Meier survival curves 73
– political stability 72–73
Conte, G. 2, 38, 68
– Conte I government 59
– Conte II government 38, 59–60
– government 32, 38, 58, 59–60
– responsibility attribution 58
– termination of governments 5–6
Cox survival analysis 11, 14, 63
– coalition complexity and government
  survival 64, 66
– Cox regression *65, 66, 67*

– stability across Republican periods 64
– survival estimates per 'Republic' *65*
CVNC *see* constructive vote of no confidence
  (CVNC)

D'Alimonte, R. 7
data codebook 93–101
DC *see* Christian Democracy (DC)
De Gasperi, A. 21, 22, 44
Diamond, L. 9
Draghi, M. 6, 58, 60, 68
– government 38, 44, 60

electoral reforms 69–71, 81, 84–85
electoral system
– mixed 28, 69–70, 77
– proportional 1, 2, 24, 69, 70, 76, 77

Fanfani, A. 51
Five Star Movement (M5S) 2
Forza Italia 2
"fragmented bipolarism" 32
Fratoianni, N. 38
– party 60

general vulnerability 31, **39–43**, 44–45, 63
Gentiloni, P. 44
governments since 1948 **33–37**
– cabinet type *49*
government termination *see* cabinet
  terminations

Hazan, R. Y. 24
Huber, J. D. 7

Improta, M. 82
instability, types of 30–32, 38, **39–43**, 44–45
institutional remedies 69
– addressing fragmentation problem 75–80
– anti-defection laws 78–80
– coalition agreements 70–71
– constructive vote of no confidence 71, 72–75

https://doi.org/10.1515/9783111329727-011

– electoral and institutional reforms 69–71, 75–80
– party discipline and defection 78–79
– party-switching regulations 78–79
– proportional representation system 69, 70, 76
– strengthening prime minister's authority 71
– uncertainty and conflict reduction 69–71
inter-party conflicts 30, 31, **39–43**, 44, 45, 63
intra-party conflicts 30, 31, **39–43**, 44, 45, 63
Israel 2, 5
– anti-defection laws 79–80
Italian Constituent Assembly 20–21
Italian constitution
– Article 67 of constitution of Italy 78
– Constitutional Bill No. (2759) 79
– Constitutional Court 25
– decentralization and regional autonomy 25–26
– government stability and motion of no confidence 24–25
– influence of international models 26
– limited executive power in 22–23
– role of political consciousness 25
Italian Left *see* Sinistra Italiana (Italian Left)
Italian Socialist Party (PSI) 20

Johnson, B. 5

Kohl, H. 7

Laakso, M. 64
Lapid, Y. 5
Lega Nord *see* Northern League (Lega Nord)
Lento, T. 24
Letta, E. 44
Lijphart, A. 7, 10
Lowell, A. L. 8, 31

M5S *see* Five Star Movement (M5S)
Mack Smith, D. 15, 16
Mair, P. 6
majoritarian systems 10
Mammarella, G. 7
marginalized government 22–23
Martelli, P. 21, 22, 23
Marzi, P. 82
Mattarella Law 81

Mattarella, S. 60
Meloni–Casellati institutional reform 81–84
Meloni, G. 38, 58, 60
Mershon, C. 9, 27
mixed electoral system 28, 69–70, 77
Morlino, L. 9
Mortati, C. 24
Müller, W. C. 13
Mussolini, B. 1, 17, 20

national identity, Italian 15–20
– anti-fascist resistance 18
– catholic church and 18
– complexities 19–20
– evolution 17
– regionalism and struggle for national unity 18–19
– role of media and popular culture 19
nation-building 3, 11, 13
Netanyahu, B. 5
no-confidence mechanism 82–83 *see also* constructive vote of no confidence (CVNC)
Northern League (Lega Nord) 19, 44

parliamentarism 24–25
Partito Comunista Italiano (PCI) 17
Partito Democratico (PD) 44
Partito Socialista Democratico Italiano (PSDI) 44
party conflicts 30, 31, 44, 45, 63, 81
party-switching regulations 78–79, 85
PCI *see* Partito Comunista Italiano (PCI)
PD *see* Partito Democratico (PD)
Pella, G. 51
"polarized multipartism" 31
policy cycle 48, 59–61
policymaking accountability 11, 47
– cabinet type *49*
– coalition bargaining *50*
– governmental agendas and policy initiatives 51–58
– policy cycle 48, 59–61
– policy discontinuity 51–58, **52–57**
– responsibility attribution 47–51, 58
Powell Jr., G. B. 9
PR electoral system *see* proportional representation electoral system (PR electoral system)

pre-unification Italy 16–17
Prodi, R. 7, 8, 44
proportional representation electoral system
    (PR electoral system) 1, 2, 24, 69, 70, 76, 77
PSDI *see* Partito Socialista Democratico Italiano
    (PSDI)
PSI *see* Italian Socialist Party (PSI)

regionalism 18–19
Renzi, M. 2, 58, 60, 73
responsibility attribution 47–51
"responsibility vs. responsiveness"
    conundrum 6
Ronzulli, L. 71
Rumor, M. 51

Salvini, M. 32, 59
Sartori, G. 7, 10, 11, 31

Shomer, Y. 13
Sinistra Italiana (Italian Left) 38, 60
Sunak, R. 5

Taagepera, R. 64
Tangentopoli 1
technical reasons 31, **39–43**, 44
technocratic leadership 38
"Third Republic" 85
Truss, M. E. 5
"tyrant syndrome" 21

"volatile tripolarism" 32

Weimar constitution 26

Zoli, A. 51

www.ingramcontent.com/pod-product-compliance
Lightning Source LLC
Chambersburg PA
CBHW031139270326
41929CB00011B/1682